HURT, JOY, AND THE GRACE OF GOD

A Resurrection Story of the Episcopal Diocese of San Joaquin, California

Jane Onstad Lamb, Editor

Foreword by Katharine Jefferts Schori,
Presiding Bishop of The Episcopal Church

APPLECART BOOKS
New York

Library of Congress Cataloging-in-Publication Data
Lamb, Jane Onstad
Hurt, Joy, and the Grace of God: a resurrection story of The Episcopal Diocese of San Joaquin, California.
2012941205

Manufactured in the United States of America
Book Design: Lee Anna Fitzgerald
Copyeditor: Jennifer Hanshaw Hackett
Proofreader: Maria Montesano Boyer

Published by Applecart Books, LLC
ISBN: 978-0615650906

This book is dedicated to the courageous Episcopalians of the Episcopal Diocese of San Joaquin who, through deep faith, a sense of humor, and hard work, were instrumental in its resurrection.

Contents

Acknowledgements

I tossed an idea out to our presiding bishop, Katharine Jefferts Schori, about writing of the experience in the reconstituted Episcopal Diocese of San Joaquin. She encouraged me to give it a try. Throughout the process Bishop Katharine has been encouraging and supportive. She has managed to teach me and correct me with humor and preciseness. Thank you: I needed the crispness of thought.

This narrative could not have been told without the contributors taking a risk and telling their stories. I admire them and I am indebted to them. They are: Marion Montgomery-Austin, Nancy Key, Richard Jennings, Cindy Smith, Juanita Weber, the Reverend Robert Woods, the Reverend Michele Racusin, The Reverend Suzy Ward, the Reverend Kathryn Galicia, the Reverend Carolyn Louise Woodall, John Ledbetter, the Reverend Glenn Kangstrom, the Reverend John Shumaker, the Reverend Dr. Tim Vivian, and the Reverend Canon Mark Hall. Thank you.

Thank you to my readers, who cleared any muddiness that crept into the manuscript. My readers were: Marla Martin Hanley, Martha Moehl, Linda Taylor, Katherine Downing Lamb, Katie Cooper, Michael Glass, and the

Reverend Robert Woods. A special thank you to Marla Martin Hanley, who enriched my knowledge of commas, but, alas, not my love of them. I would like to thank Doris Hall, the editor of *Episcopal Life San Joaquin*; a master of word flow, she died November 5, 2011. My friend and computer guru, Mary Jo Ruthven, brought me into the twenty-first century and I thank her.

Many Episcopal parishes throughout the wider church prayed for the Episcopal Diocese of San Joaquin and its rebirth. The people of the diocese gained strength from these prayers and we thank all whose prayers kept us nurtured. We especially thank the five surrounding dioceses in California, and the dioceses of Nevada and the Rio Grande for their sustaining prayers.

Without the prayers and support of our friends Ben and Linda Taylor and their son, Benjamin, we would not have been able to pursue this life-changing adventure. The Taylors daily drove across town to collect mail, check on the house, and order the required maintenance for an empty home. We will forever be indebted to them.

I thank, with deep love and admiration, my husband, the Right Reverend Jerry A. Lamb, for his encouragement, occasional necessary wording, and constant support. Kate, our daughter, often called me in the morning to get my day started with a giggle and a breath of fresh air. I can't forget to thank my blood pressure reducer, Marky, our Australian shepherd, who kept me laughing.

None of this would have happened without the good advice and hard work of my editor, Nancy Fitzgerald. The story of San Joaquin would not have been published without her and I would like to acknowledge her great help.

Las Cruces, New Mexico
January 2012

Foreword

The story of San Joaquin is like that of many human communities—it is filled with pain, love, betrayal, good and faithful work, and relationships that both delight and frustrate. It is above all a paschal story—abundant dying, desertion, hopelessness, and resurrection. The human road home to God takes the same journey Jesus did.

It can be disconcerting to discover that church communities have all-too-human failings, but they wouldn't be truly human communities if they didn't. Churches and cathedrals, chapels and temples all exhibit the same messy behavior we encounter in other parts of our lives. This story is important because it tells of the ability of people who feel abandoned to remember or discover that God is still in their midst, even when they have lost most of what they thought defined their lives with God.

As you read, don't go looking for villains and heroes. Pogo said it well some decades ago: They is us. Go looking for faithful and creative responses to the unexpected—find the Spirit doing new things in old vessels, and bringing new and unexpected partners in the midst of crisis.

This is the story of a church being vulnerable enough to let itself be re-created, to show the world what it looks like to rise from the dead. The story isn't finished, however. But it just might give hope to others who feel betrayed or abandoned. We live in a time of seismic shifts in social structures, including what it looks like to be a church or faith community. The spiritual maturity and grace to walk into that terror-filled land of shifting ground can bring new and abundant life to those who are willing to travel light, receive hospitality from others, and offer themselves for the healing of the world. Blessings on your own journey!

Katharine Jefferts Schori
New York, New York
February 2012

The Hurts

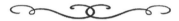

"I lift my eyes to the hills; from where is my help to come?
My help comes from the Lord; the maker of heaven and earth."
Psalm 121, Book of Common Prayer, 1979

The distance from the bishop's office of the Episcopal Diocese of Northern California and the church farthest to the north in the Episcopal Diocese of San Joaquin was about thirty miles. In 2007, the two dioceses were also about thirty years apart. My husband was bishop of Northern California for fifteen and a half years and I watched with sadness the isolation of the Episcopal Diocese of San Joaquin from The Episcopal Church. In December of 2007, the majority of the clergy and laity of the Diocese of San Joaquin voted to leave The Episcopal Church and join the Province of the Southern Cone, which includes dioceses in Argentina, Bolivia, Chile, Paraguay, Peru, and Uruguay.

For my husband and me, the break was especially poignant because we were married in the Diocese of San

Joaquin, at the historic St. James Church in Sonora, where my father was rector. On that day in 1971, I never imagined that Jerry would one day become the provisional bishop of San Joaquin.

We retired to Las Cruces, New Mexico, in January of 2007 after my husband resigned as bishop of Northern California, but nine days later he was off to the Diocese of Nevada as interim bishop while they searched for their new bishop. Their preceding bishop, Katharine Jefferts Schori, had been elected presiding bishop of The Episcopal Church at the 2006 General Convention in Columbus, Ohio. As the position of interim bishop was a half-time position, I stayed in Las Cruces, learning about our new environment, making new friends, and settling into our parish home. My husband flew to and from Nevada about every two weeks during that year.

In January 2008, Dan Edwards was ordained bishop of Nevada, and Jerry and I happily settled into our second retirement. But it was to be short-lived again. Just a month earlier, in December 2007, the Diocese of San Joaquin had voted illegally for the second time to leave The Episcopal Church. This sham vote was held in an attempt to satisfy the Constitutions and Canons of The Episcopal Church requiring two votes to enact a constitutional change. In February of 2008 conversations began between the presiding bishop's office and my husband about his possible role in the Episcopal Diocese of San Joaquin.

At a special convention in March 2008, my husband was elected and installed as provisional bishop of the Episcopal Diocese of San Joaquin. The night before the convention there was a reception at St. Anne's Episcopal Church in Stockton. A good number from the youth group was there to help, and I heard three teenage boys run down a hall with all the excitement of meeting a major league baseball star. Whispering, "The lady bishop is here, the lady bishop is here!" they pushed in front of me, not out of rudeness but sheer elation. Before them was Presiding Bishop Katharine, not only the first woman bishop many people in this diocese had ever seen, but the first woman presiding bishop in The Episcopal Church. The entire assemblage was thrilled to meet her and reconnect with House of Deputies President Bonnie Anderson. After Evening Prayer there was a time for questions and answers. The evening was full of hope and anticipation and thoughtful questions. The atmosphere in the church was electric with enthusiasm and expectation. The following day the special convention took place at St. John's Episcopal Church in Lodi.

This is the story of the journey of the influential group Remain Episcopal and the reconstituted Episcopal Diocese of San Joaquin, California. A great part of my heart has been with the people of San Joaquin, and I love and admire them greatly. It has been an honor to be part of their story.

As a moderate Episcopalian, I was troubled to learn that a number of unnecessary "hurts" had occurred in the past two decades in the Diocese of San Joaquin. Though Episcopalians there were exhausted spiritually and emotionally, they were determined that no one would take their church away from them. In this book, I'd like to name the hurts and express the surprising, concomitant joys. Others who have contributed to this book will share their own accounts of resurrection, for this book will be a story of resurrection, not of blame.

The overwhelming hurts include: betrayal, absolute authority, clericalism, censorship of information, fraud, isolation, spiritual hurt, ostracism, abandonment, and greed. The hurts were overlapping. Try to imagine all the pain going on at the same time; every part of the San Joaquin Episcopal Church body was aching together.

Every bishop, priest, and deacon makes a promise at ordination, and usually once a year thereafter: " ... and I do solemnly engage to conform to the doctrine, discipline and worship of The Episcopal Church." (Book of Common Prayer, 1979, 513, 526, 538)

It is a well-defined, straightforward promise. It doesn't say anything about "maybe." One can certainly leave the church with no strings attached, choosing to re-nounce one's orders of ministry in the church if one can no longer "engage to conform to the doctrine, discipline and worship of The Episcopal Church." But being disloyal to the doctrine, discipline, and worship of The Episcopal Church while maintaining one's Holy Orders in the Episco-pal Church is *betrayal*. It was clear to me the people of San Joaquin who chose to remain in the Church felt a deep sense of betrayal by the bishop and clergy who abandoned The Episcopal Church.

One of the stories we heard when we first arrived in the Diocese of San Joaquin was what those aligned with the Southern Cone perceived The Episcopal Church to believe. We were told by a number of people that they had heard or seen laminated pew cards pronouncing the following about The Episcopal Church:

> That we do not believe in the Trinity.
> That we believe the Resurrection is a myth.
> That we believe the virgin birth is fiction.
> That The Episcopal Church does not consider
> baptism necessary.

All of that, of course, is false. To proclaim those ideas as fact is a betrayal of the very promise made at ordination. The remaining Episcopalians, trying to be faithful to the church, found these accusations confusing, deceptive, and frightening. The accusations were *fraud*, pure and simple.

Absolute authority corrupts absolutely—clear, simple, and true. When only one person, or very few people, has all the power and there is no room for discussion or dissention, there is unequal power. *Clericalism* is a partner to absolute authority. It is the practice of the clergy, mostly male except for a few female deacons, retaining all the power, leaving the laity with little say in important decisions. In fact, only a few laity had significant impact on diocesan affairs. Couple *censorship of information*—keeping knowledge of the wider church from clergy and laity—with absolute authority and clericalism and you end up with *isolation*. There were other ways, I learned, to create a sense of isolation, and in the Diocese of San Joaquin all of these were put to use: silent clergy retreats, discouraging clergy spouses from interacting with one another, and maintaining a constant sense of siege.

Much of the laity of the Episcopal Diocese of San Joaquin was unaware that there was a monthly newspaper published by The Episcopal Church called *Episcopal Life*. Other Episcopal publications such as *Forward Day by Day*, as well as Episcopal websites explaining programs and ministries offering a wider view of The Episcopal Church, were unknown as well. The diocese was isolated. Some, though, were aware of the contrast between San Joaquin and the wider church beyond its borders. It is interesting to note that clergy who were knowledgeable about wider church matters and had served in other dioceses and were concerned by the imbalance of power were the ones who remained in The Episcopal Church.

And all of this leads us to the spiritual health of the diocese.

One's sense of the Spirit is as personal and as deep as one's soul. If this sense of spirituality is dismissed, ma-

nipulated, or allowed to be expressed only in a certain pre-
scribed way, there is sure to be *spiritual hurt.* Spiritual hurt
can play havoc with a person's relationship to God and with
others in the Church, the parish, and the wider Christian
community. Spiritual hurt can be detrimental to one's overall health.

In the Diocese of San Joaquin, there were many forms
of spiritual hurt. Many Episcopalians, or those who wished
to be Episcopalians, felt a vivid sense of ostracism because
of their race, sexual orientation, gender, or socio-economic
standing. Episcopalians who did not wish to separate from
The Episcopal Church were made to feel inferior. Some
were asked to leave their church; some tried to stay but finally left, with a deep sense of hurt and abandonment. Except for attendance at General Convention, there was a dis-
connect between The Episcopal Church in San Joaquin and
the wider Episcopal Church. There may have been contact
with other clergy and other dioceses, but not with the larger
church. And when, in December 2007, the diocese held the
sham vote to leave The Episcopal Church altogether, those
who were left behind experienced an overwhelming sense
of *abandonment.*

One of the more egregious hurts was the closing of
churches; property was sold, and clergy and parishioners
were locked out of their spiritual homes. At one church, the
locks were changed so suddenly that at the last minute the
Christmas Eve service had to be canceled. The priest was
not given a set of keys to the new locks, and the church was
subsequently sold. This is the hurt of *greed.* It is the conten-
tion of the Episcopalians of the Episcopal Diocese of San
Joaquin that all properties that were San Joaquin Episcopal
properties before the schism belong in the hands of The
Episcopal Church. At the present time, these properties are
being held by the Anglican Diocese of San Joaquin and are

subject to litigation.

Though I've catalogued the hurts that caused pain, spiritual torment, emotional exhaustion, and financial hardship on the Episcopal Diocese of San Joaquin, in the chapters that follow, others will share stories of their own. But as Christians, we know with all our hearts that the hurts and the pains are never the end of the story. We are people of resurrection. Our diocese has emerged on the other side of hurt to experience joy and a healthy diocese, wonderfully resurrected.

Las Cruces, New Mexico
January 2011

Wormwood's Triumph

Marion Montgomery-Austin

Marion Montgomery-Austin is an active member of the Episco-pal Diocese of San Joaquin. She serves as the chair of the Com-mission on Ministry and is on the vestry at Holy Family Episcopal Church in Fresno. She believes that as the most architecturally beautiful cities in the world are those that were rebuilt after di-sasters, the joy and challenge of rebuilding The Episcopal Church in the Episcopal Diocese of San Joaquin will be a glory to God.

This is the story of a tragedy, the victory of evil over good. The characters in the tragedy are all too human with their virtues and foibles, so bent on self-destruction for high and moral reasons. The main character here, around whom the story centers, is Bishop John-David Schofield. When I think of John-David, I try to remember the kind and engag-ing man who almost made me burn the fancy dinner I had prepared for his visit. He had discovered my four-year-old watching *Bambi* in the den (to keep her from underfoot), pulled her onto his lap, and watched the entire movie with the same fascination she had. Turns out, he had never seen it before.

I try to remember the man who acted as my husband's confessor and brought him through a spiritual crisis and into a deeper and greater faith. The man who wore his collar and cross whenever he traveled so that he was visible to any stranger with a question about Jesus and who shared anecdotes about these encounters, always laughing that it was the most unlikely looking stranger who presented the toughest theological challenges. The man who loved Jesus with his whole heart and mind and wanted to share that love with the whole world.

He loved to entertain, spending hours with his cook, Leilani, planning menus and shopping lists. An evening in his home always began with a tour of his beautiful, historic house, and always moved on to cocktails, music, and wonderful conversation. He was charming, intelligent, and engaging, and he was a man of very strong conviction. I remember vividly one evening as we were sitting at table, he suddenly took my hand and told me earnestly, "I want you to understand I like and respect women. I would be the first to vote for a woman president. I just can't ordain them."

At John-David's invitation, I served a four-year term on the diocesan Commission on Ministry (COM). He was emphatic and clear in his message and charge to us. While he would not personally ordain women, he would not block their path to ordination. His COM should consider women equal in all ways to male applicants and let them know that at the appropriate time, he would help to make sure they would be ordained by other bishops. Readily acknowledging that his views on women's ordination were his own, he promised to remain open to the Holy Spirit to move him on this issue, as it had on the issue of divorced persons. I believed him.

After being active in my parish for many years, being asked to serve on COM exposed me to the workings and politics of the diocese. The experience of helping raise up new clergy for the church and shepherding them through the twists and turns of a discernment process was challenging and rewarding, and I loved it. After my term on COM ended, I said yes when asked to run for election to the SC. It was commonly known that my personal views were much more liberal than most in the diocese but I was by no means alone and had always been treated with respect.

It was only after I became a member of the SC that things started to change. Rumors began to swirl around the diocese about the bishop and what his intentions toward The Episcopal Church might be. Various blogs on the Internet began to publish and discuss any bit of gossip coming out of San Joaquin. About this time, my dinner invitations stopped and the engaging, genial bishop I had known became increasingly distant, cold, and formal. He had always had a bit of a "chip on his shoulder" and was sensitive to criticism of any kind but now the proverbial chip had become a log that visibly weighed him down. He often seemed angry and impatient with differing points of view.

At the SC meetings, the members—four lay and four clergy—discussed and voted on whether or not other dioceses should hold elections for new bishops. I was surprised to find that the committee had few responsibilities: vote to approve or disapprove the election of bishops in other dioceses serving The Episcopal Church, approve applicants at various stages as they moved toward ordination, and approve any real estate transactions in our own diocese. Occasionally, we'd be asked to vote to approve the election of a controversial bishop in another diocese, and lively conversation would ensue as to what our specific role was: Were we voting on the person's qualifications to be a bishop or on whether or not the election had been fairly conducted in accordance with canon law?

Very rarely, a parish would want to sell or purchase real estate and would need our permission. It was obvious that we were considered a rubber-stamp committee; we received minimum information, always at the last minute. I remember one poor rector who had been discussing the details of a sale with the bishop's office for months and no one had mentioned that the SC needed to be consulted. At the last minute the escrow agent noticed in the deed that the SC would have to sign off. The parish was selling an old rectory, the rector was buying a new home, and the new buyer, having already sold his home, was ready to move in. This was all happening over Christmas and we had two days to come to a decision and get our written permission to the escrow agent or the deal would fall apart. The rector of the parish was almost apoplectic that we had to be consulted at all, much less that we had the power to ruin everyone's Christmas. We continually felt disrespected and abused as a committee.

After six months of these mundane, boring meetings, I called the president of the SC, who happened to be my parish priest, and demanded to know—only half in jest—where the secret meetings were being held and when was I going to get invited. He sighed and said there were no secret meetings; this is all there was to being on the SC. The bishop attended the meetings, with rare exception—usually when he wanted our quick vote on a real estate transaction he'd already approved. He once lamented to us that one of his brother bishops had been bragging that his SC was like a "circle of angels" and how he wished we were more like that for him. We stared at each other, aghast. How could we be a circle of angels when he never met or shared information with us? We felt like children, rebuked and rejected for no fault we could understand. What were we doing wrong if we were never asked to do anything at all?

As it turned out, he had good cause for keeping the Standing Committee well away from his plans to break from The Episcopal Church. The four clergy on the SC were rectors of the largest and most affluent parishes in the diocese; while they were all conservative men, they had no interest in leaving The Episcopal Church. They differed in opinion about the ordination of women—two for and two against—but despite their conservative points of view, none were interested in tearing the diocese apart and rocking the boats of their very comfortable congregations. The other lay members were similar—some conservative, some not, all trying hard to stay above the rumors and gossip swirling around them.

At one meeting, Bishop Schofield surprised us, arriving with great excitement, clutching a roll of blueprints. The real estate market was booming, he said, and we had a great opportunity to make some additions to our Episcopal Conference Center, Oakhurst (ECCO). He had received an offer from a local developer to purchase some of our prime acreage, near the public road, for almost one million dollars and he wanted our approval for the sale. The plans he brought to show us were of a meeting hall to be built in the heart of the ECCO campus.

We knew that ECCO had wonderful dormitory space, a dining hall, and a chapel, but it lacked classrooms. The bishop explained that we were missing out on renting to small conventions because of our lack of break-out space, so he had been working personally with the architects to design a flexible space that could accommodate both small and large groups. He was particularly excited about a new type of soundproof movable wall.

We obligingly looked at the blueprints, and heads

nodded as he explained the need for more meeting space. Though we were initially suspicious of his intentions, he specifically and personally assured us that every dime of the property sale would go only into the new construction and any overage would be added to the Episcopal Conference Center Foundation for future improvements. The sale was approved unanimously and we were pleased that ECCO would be improved. It was the right sale at the right time for all the right reasons. It was more than a year later before it dawned on me that no new improvements were ever made at ECCO and no deposits made to the Foundation. The new building for the conference center was never mentioned again.

Rumors of our diocese seceding from The Episcopal Church continued to build. SC members all obsessively read the numerous blogs every morning and called one another to share disparate bits of gossip. But we were out of the loop, with no real information about what was going on. Discouraged and increasingly angry, I met with the SC president and told him I was thinking of resigning. He asked me to stay on—a moderate voice was needed on the SC and if I left I'd be replaced with a hard-line conservative. So I stayed.

For the first time, at our regular meetings we began to discuss openly the rumors and potential consequences of what a split might mean. This was difficult conversation for all of us, particularly the clergy. We even talked at one meeting about reaching out to the presiding bishop for help in stopping Schofield. The more we read canon law and tried to find a way forward, the more we came to realize that unless we were willing to bring a presentment against our bishop, we had no other recourse, and we had no proof to justify a presentment. We worried about what The Episcopal Church leaders might do if we asked them to step in—or even if they'd be able or willing to help us.

We began to pressure Bishop Schofield, in person and in writing, to give us more information and tell us what he was planning. He reluctantly agreed to allow the president of our Standing Committee to sit in on a few meetings and to be involved at the fringes, with the strict caveat that he was not to share any information with any other SC member. Sadly, that old high-school desire to be included with the big boys was strong enough for our president to jump at the offer. The rest of the SC members were left feeling frustrated and even more hopeless. We were no longer a united group; our moment to act had passed.

We began to suspect that the financial structure of the diocese was hinky—money was not going where it was supposed to. We suspected a war chest was being put together to fund future litigation, but we couldn't identify specifics. Financial statements were not available and the books were only open to two or three people close to the bishop. The Standing Committee became increasingly concerned and began to write letters to the bishop and his staff requesting copies of financial reports. Feeling completely ignored, our requests became more demanding and finally even threatening. In the end, the bishop agreed to attend our next meeting and answer our financial questions. He arrived with his attorney. After he opened with prayer, the bishop turned to his attorney and said, "Please tell them." We were informed that we had no legal right whatsoever to any financial information and that we were not to ask questions about anything other than those specific areas of responsibility allowed to us by canon law. I resigned from the Standing Committee the next day.

Heartsick over the situation, I did not attend the final Diocesan Convention and even stayed away from my own parish. I wanted to be anywhere but in the middle of this terrible strife. Late one afternoon while out shopping,

I received a call from one of the clergy still on the Standing Committee. He was frantic; they had just heard that the presiding bishop intended to dissolve the current SC and "take over the diocese." He wanted to let the presiding bishop know that he and the other clergy on the SC did not want to leave The Episcopal Church; they wanted to continue on as the Episcopal Diocese of San Joaquin and simply let Schofield go his own way.

As a group, the clergy on the Standing Committee represented four of the largest parishes in the diocese, and felt that they could sway a significant number of other parishes to stand with them and simply stay in The Episcopal Church. Letting Schofield go to the Southern Cone was a wonderful way to "get him out of the way," they reasoned, something he'd wanted to do for some time. My friend asked if I'd be willing to make a few phone calls and try to initiate a dialogue with the presiding bishop's office.

I spent the next two hours talking with the attorney representing the presiding bishop's office. It was one of the most frustrating conversations I've ever had. It was a cold and windy day so I kept walking around the department store, animatedly talking on my cell phone to the amusement of those passing by. The attorney felt that if they left the Standing Committee in control of the diocese, they would help facilitate Bishop Schofield's plans to take property and eventually follow him to the Southern Cone.

Increasingly frustrated, I tried to explain how strained the relationship was between the Standing Committee and the bishop, how getting rid of Schofield was exactly what they'd wanted all along, how they wanted to deliver the four largest parishes and an undetermined number of other churches to The Episcopal Church without controversy. We just wanted our diocese back the way it was before Schofield began his campaign for schism, I insisted to the attorney.

I asked if the presiding bishop would speak directly with the members of the Standing Committee but the request was declined. Finally I was directly told that the presiding bishop and staff simply did not believe me.

When I explained to the clergy on the Standing Committee that they were not believed or trusted, they became angry. All the old fears about The Episcopal Church leaders came flooding back. Schofield had repeatedly warned us all that there was no room in the larger Episcopal Church for a conservative diocese, that the views of conservative clergy and parishioners would never be respected, that conservatives would be marginalized or thrown out of their churches. In particular, the SC saw the coming takeover by the presiding bishop as heavy handed and illegal.

The Standing Committee insisted that they were the legal representative of the diocese in the absence of a bishop. As they saw it, our bishop had absented himself and after all these years the Standing Committee was finally to be in control. The fear was that the incoming "jack boots" (clergy words, not mine) would marginalize them in retribution for Schofield's past sins. To compound the problem, the clergy watched as the leadership of the diocese passed into the hands of a small, strident, liberal group of people who had long stood in vocal opposition to the diocesan leadership.

Could the situation have been handled differently? Yes. Would it have made a difference in the long run? Perhaps. The real tragedy here doesn't lie in buildings and properties lost to The Episcopal Church. The real tragedy lies in the broken relationships among the people who worshiped in those buildings. I will always believe that a more gracious and Christian response from The Episcopal Church leaders would have been far better for all concerned. We might have lost a few buildings, but we might have kept more hearts.

For many years, here in San Joaquin, the ultra-conservative and the ultra-liberal sat together, side by side, each Sunday. We raised our children together; we mourned each other's losses and chatted at coffee hour. It was the uncommon grace and beauty of The Episcopal Church that we could worship together, celebrate what we shared in common, and be in community. That sense of peace and harmony is gone. In the tumult, whether you wanted to or not, you were forced to pick a side, stand and be counted in the fight. People I love now look the other way when we pass. It breaks my heart every time it happens.

It's tempting to heap all the blame on one man, John-David Schofield, whose ego and sense of his own righteousness led us to into such a terrible schism. It's true that he carefully spent years building a haven for like-minded clergy and systematically eliminating from leadership anyone who did not agree with him, distancing those he could not control. But he did not do this alone. Every single person involved bears a responsibility in this terrible schism. Large or small, we all played a part.

So much evil has been done in San Joaquin, I question whether it is worth the effort to try to rebuild from the debris and bitter feelings that are left. Neither side is financially able to survive without significant outside support. Splitting our diocese and merging the pieces with neighboring dioceses makes sense to me. Becoming a small part of a healthy, functioning diocese with resources and traditions to share would go a long way toward healing our wounds and making us feel a part of The Episcopal Church.

I keep imagining that Wormwood of the C. S. Lewis tale, *The Screwtape Letters*, would be rejoicing over his great triumph in San Joaquin. This tragedy would certainly guarantee him a grand promotion.

Fresno, California
July 2011

How Did This Happen?

Mark Hall

The Reverend Canon Mark Hall was canon to the ordinary for the Episcopal Diocese of San Joaquin for the first three years of the reconstituted diocese. He is now enjoying a well-deserved retirement. Canon Hall has been in the Diocese of San Joaquin for twenty-seven years and possesses a wealth of knowledge about the diocese that proved invaluable to its resurrection.

In early 2007, after the first vote at Diocesan Convention to disaffiliate from The Episcopal Church, the organization Remain Episcopal sponsored an event for loyal Episcopalians at St. John's Parish in Lodi, with Bonnie Anderson, president of the Episcopal House of Deputies, as our featured speaker. In a small-group meeting with Bonnie, after she listened to our stories, she asked, "Would you consider that you have been a victim of spiritual abuse?"

I couldn't answer the question immediately, though others agreed. I had trouble getting my mind around the idea that I was a victim. I had stood up to Bishop Schofield.

I had spoken up at convention. I had helped found Remain Episcopal and was one of the key clergy leading the opposition. But on reflection I had to admit that I—like many others—had been a victim of unholy actions that abused spiritual trust.

I came to the diocese in 1979 while I was on active duty in the Air Force as a navigator. I had completed seminary prior to going on active duty, and had been ordained in Maine while serving at Loring Air Force Base. When I completed my active duty commitment in 1980, Bishop Rivera, then bishop of the Episcopal Diocese of San Joaquin, asked me to help with fundraising for the Episcopal Conference Center, Oakhurst (ECCO). After a few months of that, the bishop asked me to serve as his canon to the ordinary, which I did for almost a year. The Air Force reassigned my wife (who was still on active duty) back to Maine, so I didn't return to the diocese until 1987 after the failure of that marriage. I initially served as vicar of St. Alban's, Los Banos. My previous experience in the diocese also quickly earned me positions on the ECCO board and the Diocesan Finance Committee. A year later, the bishop appointed me chairman of the Diocesan Education Commission.

What was the diocese like prior to the election of John-David Schofield as bishop? Reflecting the Central Valley values, it was conservative but surprisingly diverse. Among the clergy there was open debate and exchange of ideas. People looked forward to conventions and clergy conferences. But as diverse as we were, we were clergy together, following our bishop's emphasis on growth and mission. Admittedly, we were a bit of a backwater diocese, and the stipends were below average, but there was a sense of unity. We were The Episcopal Church in the San Joaquin Valley. As wild and wacky as the clergy were, we were only out of sync with the broader church because we didn't have any women in priestly orders.

At the electing convention for a coadjutor, Bishop Rivera was bound and determined to elect someone opposed to the ordination of women. Though he later rued his actions, he pushed for the election of Schofield, the only remaining candidate who fit that standard. The laity did not seem content with that decision, but it was late in the evening and they were tired so they went along with the slight clergy majority. Barely two-thirds of all delegates, clergy and laity, signed the consent forms. I was not one of them. I called Schofield a few days after the election to congratulate him, and also allowed as I didn't sign the consent forms, as did a great many other clergy and laity. I believed I owed it to him to give him a "heads-up" concerning the difficulties of the election and the division in the diocese. Little did I know that from that day onward, I was identified as an enemy.

Shortly after I moved to be rector of Trinity, Madera, in 1991, concerned that women priests had been barred from even speaking in the diocese, let alone celebrating the sacraments, I coauthored a document called *Good Order in the Church*. It argued that a bishop has a right to have a conscientious objection to the ordination of women, but he still has to obey the canons and allow women to serve in the diocese if they are called as clergy. It also asserted that General Convention establishes the norms for The Episcopal Church, not the local bishop. The ban on women clergy was the start of a series of events, programs, and actions that distanced the diocese from the broader church and from General Convention. Bishop Schofield aligned himself with other like-minded bishops, and a campaign of alienation from The Episcopal Church progressed. In the beginning, there were enough clergy to oppose this direction. After a few years, replacement clergy were dependent on the bishop, so the laity opposed these actions. However, after General Convention 2003, the Diocesan Convention voted to cut off all funds to the General Convention budget and they further voted to include a "partial accession" clause in the constitution of the diocese. This meant that the diocese would reserve the right to reject any teachings or actions of General Convention with which it did not agree. It was shortly after this that Father Rick Matters and I met with Michael Glass, and, along with mostly laity, we formed Remain Episcopal.

By now the diocese had been transformed. Everything to do with The Episcopal Church was criticized; the clergy were divided into those who were "in favor" and those who were "out." Loyalty to the bishop was the only criteria. Power in the diocese became concentrated in fewer hands, and conventions became more structured and orchestrated. We were presented with twisted logic, the system became closed, and secrets abounded. Our once open-ended and fun clergy conferences were transformed into silent retreats with carefully chosen speakers. Isolated and marginalized, I lost track of where people stood. I no longer held positions in diocesan governance. There were fewer and fewer of the old guard clergy.

In 1995 I was fed up with the diocese, but I had three children in high school. Out of the blue I was offered a teaching position at Madera High School and I accepted. I did some supply work for a few friends but later found that I'd been removed from the clergy supply list. I also continued to volunteer at Camp San Joaquin Music Camp, which was part of the Diocese of San Joaquin camp program, and one summer directed the camp and rebuilt most of the Long House. I was never recognized for the summer-long volunteer position as camp director, or for saving thousands of dollars on renovations. Actually, a few years later, I was falsely accused of mismanaging funds and for conduct unbecoming an ordained person. Even the Standing Committee members who investigated did not understand why I was being charged.

Because of my Air Force Reserve duty and my involvement in some larger church conferences, I had the opportunity to experience the church outside the diocese, and it was always a breath of fresh air. But I was enmeshed in a dysfunctional system. When I tried to explain to those outside the system, I did not feel understood. I could not convince people what it was really like. It's hard to understand from outside the dysfunctional system. There were times when even I doubted things were as bad as I perceived them. But over and over again, something would happen to reinforce my experience.

In 1999, after my youngest graduated from high school, I began looking for work outside the diocese. I came close to being called to several parishes, but Susan, my wife, had difficulty with the locations of a few, and after reflection I wasn't willing to go to others. Although I was asked to be interim at St. Anne's in Stockton, I was planning to leave the diocese at some point. However, their search broke down after their candidates refused to serve with Bishop Schofield, and after a second search committee was formed— and I had moved on to help start a charter school—Bishop Schofield permitted my name to go forward as a candidate for rector. When I was chosen, he tried to dissuade the vestry and search committee with erroneous information about me. They stuck to their decision and I became rector in 2002.

St. Anne's was an unusual parish in the diocese, as a number of members were involved at the broader church level, and there were at least thirty graduates of EfM (Education for Ministry). It was the only church in the diocese with the program. I was rector of a congregation that was informed, supportive of The Episcopal Church, and steeped in the Episcopal ethos. I may have been in a theological wasteland of a diocese, but my parish was a Garden of Eden.

It was from this platform that I was able to be involved in the Remain Episcopal movement. Father Rick Matters and I met with Michael Glass in 2003 and began the conversation about how we could counter the move for separation that was clearly developing. Michael Glass is the chancellor of the Episcopal Diocese of San Joaquin and was the attorney for Remain Episcopal. Father Rick Matters was rector of St. John's, Lodi, a healthy, vibrant parish instrumental in Remain Episcopal. The Remain Episcopal group was just getting started and getting connected with other groups in dioceses where separatist activity was fomenting. Remain Episcopal was a mostly lay-led group with leaders like Nancy Key, Cindy Smith, and Marshall Johnson. Just a few clergy were willing to be involved.

It wasn't until the clergy conference in 2006, after the first vote to disassociate from The Episcopal Church, that a larger and surprisingly diverse group of clergy met off site. From this group developed the core clergy that stayed with The Episcopal Church. Though we were few in numbers, it was a change to have fellow clergy support after such a long time of isolation. The two events that marked a new spring for the diocese were the open meeting and celebration with Bonnie Anderson in Lodi in January 2007, and the wonderful and affirming coming together of Episcopalians in Hanford after the second vote. In both cases we had well over three hundred persons gathered to affirm The Episcopal Church in the San Joaquin Valley. It was an indication that we were not alone: There was support within and without the diocese, and we were going to Remain Episcopal.

From the time of the second vote to disassociate in

December 2007, I became a key member of the steering committee, mostly made up of Remain Episcopal members, who began the process of planning and implementing the special meeting of the convention to reconstitute the diocese and approve Bishop Jerry Lamb as provisional bishop. It was a heady and very busy time. The parish supported me by hiring a part-time assistant, the Reverend Lyn Morlan, who, after I was appointed canon to the ordinary, became priest-in-charge. She is now rector of St. Anne's.

From December 2007 until after the special convention at the end of March 2008, we were working twelve or more hours a day, having multiple phone conferences, and finding our way through a lot of confusion as we charted new waters. What had seemed unthinkable to so many outside the diocese was now reality. Initially, our "offices" were a combination of St. Anne's, Michael Glass's office, and cyberspace. In the beginning of March, we acquired office space at the Congregational Church and scouted out desks, a copy machine, and even staplers. We were starting from scratch.

With the presiding bishop and so many supporters from neighboring dioceses, the special convention was truly wonderful. We put together a quorum consisting of one-third of congregations and clergy in good standing, and I was appointed by the presiding bishop to be the presiding officer. It was the only convention I have ever attended where every vote was unanimous and there was no discussion. We were all so glad to have our diocese back, although we were painfully aware that this was just the start of the process of reclamation and renewal.

The change in the diocese was palpable. We now had a sense of solidarity. We were all insiders. We had our church back again. We were being supported from all over the church. We began the process of empowering the laity

again with a commitment to shared leadership and authority. There was truth and openness once again. The clarity of
the Good News was there.

Of course there were rocky spots. One of these was
the financial condition of the diocese, which consisted of
about one quarter of parishes and communicants. Most of
our congregations were displaced from their properties;
Bishop Lamb and the Standing Committee began the painful process of deposing clergy. Departing clergy refused to
talk to us, or to affirm that they were no longer Episcopalians and had taken manifest steps to abandon the church,
so we really didn't have a choice. Yet for me, it was difficult
to process all that paperwork, and to feel so separated from
those with whom I'd served.

I went to my first General Convention as a deputy in
2009. Two things in particular stand out for me from that
experience. One was the public narrative training. It was
so important to learn to tell our story: the story of the diocese and the story of the Gospel. The other was the Episcopal Identity Project. I knew that the primary reason for the
split in our diocese, and dioceses such as Pittsburg and Fort
Worth, was that people had lost sight of or been led astray
from a clear vision of what it means to be an Episcopalian. I
was so pleased to share my story, and listen as so many others told what it means to belong to and be embraced by our
church.

Somewhere in the turmoil of the first few months
of rebuilding, the Reverend Terry Martin, in the persona
of Father Jake in his "Father Jake Stops the World" blog,
published a response from Mary Clara in February 2008 in
an article entitled "The Schismatic Bully": [1]

> We know that many factors have contributed to the
> current movement to split the Church and create

some form of international disciplinary authority for Anglicanism. Disagreements about doctrine and governance, differences in cultural practices and beliefs, personal ambition, power struggles, subversion and funding from outside parties, reverberations from colonial and missionary history, and other causes have been discussed at great length. What I haven't seen is much attention to psychological factors, and specifically to the psychology of bullying. Where bizarre thinking and behavior have been observed in a particular place over a period of many years, leading to a catastrophic outcome, the possibility should be considered that a critical factor in the entire drama has been the success of a disordered individual in gaining a position of power and using it to play out on a grand scale his own internal need to split the world into pure and impure, good and evil, true and false, faithful and treasonous, saved and damned, orthodox and apostate/heretical.

The author, Mary Clara, is addressing a difficult subject for Episcopalians: evil. We know what the fruits of the Spirit are. Bishop Schofield produced quite the opposite. The mystery for me is why so many intelligent, educated individuals follow him and blindly support him. Were they duped, manipulated, cajoled, hoodwinked, and brainwashed? Or was something else at work? We have been too tolerant of inappropriate actions and leadership on both sides of the spectrum. Unwilling to name the sin, we allowed evil to flourish. In the process, though, we have learned the lesson

[1] http://frjakestopstheworld.blogspot.com/2008/02/schismatic-bully.html. Used with permission.

as a Church that I hope we will not soon forget. The Gospel deserves better from us.

Stockton, California
March 2011

Remain Episcopal

Nancy Key

Nancy Key is a layperson who was instrumental in question-ing the response of the diocese and bishop after the General Convention of 2003 approved Gene Robinson, an openly gay bishop, and the subsequent schism of the diocese over this matter. She is co-founder of Remain Episcopal and is chair of the General Convention delegates from the Episcopal Diocese of San Joaquin. Remain Episcopal was the organization that kept a connection to The Episcopal Church and played a part in the diocese's rebuilding.

It was a warm Saturday in August 2003 and at my parish, there was to be a report on General Convention. I had work to do—work important to my business—and I really needed to stay at my office. But a friend—an Episcopal priest from the Diocese of California—said I must go.

First the back-story. Those days, the mood of the leadership in the Diocese of San Joaquin was one of op-position to The Episcopal Church. True, they called them-selves Episcopalians, but they insisted that true believers must accept their tenets: that ordained priesthood and indeed all ecclesiastical and secular power was reserved for men and that gay and lesbian people were sinful and in need of healing. In my own parish, St. Columba's in Fresno, I'd heard the associate priest declare that The Episcopal Church had lost its way, that it was not adhering to the Instruments of Communion, and that it was headed for expulsion from the Anglican Communion. This was heavy news for me—I'd only recently come back into the Episcopal fold—but it was also hard to believe.

I'd been a cradle Episcopalian, active in the church through my early twenties, but I joined the Methodist Church when I married because I wanted my family to worship together. The fact that I didn't stand by my own faith illustrates my lack of gumption in those days. I was not a trouble-maker, or even a wave-maker. But in 2001 I attended a wedding of some dear friends at St. Columba's. The wonderful Episcopal service, the liturgy, and the theology so embraced me that I immediately came back. I joined the inquirers' class and renewed my membership in The Episcopal Church.

The congregation at St. Columba was a happy one—coffee hour after church was pleasant, and though I attended classes, the theological divide I would eventually identify wasn't immediately apparent. My knowledge of the growing schism in The Episcopal Church came more from reading newspaper articles about the upcoming election of Gene Robinson than from coffee-hour chats. However, after the people of New Hampshire elected Gene Robinson as their bishop, the intensity of the conversation at my own parish escalated. There were several meetings prior to General Convention in which the rector and associate made presentations. While I celebrated Gene's election, the clergy of St. Columba's, and indeed the members of the congregation, deplored it as abhorrent in the eyes of God. Although there were measured questions, no one opposed the views of the leadership and clergy at those meetings. I sat quietly, blissfully unaware of the diocesan mood. In those days, my knowledge of Episcopal matters was limited to my own parish and what I read in the paper about the larger church, to which our diocese seemed to have little connection. *Episcopal Life* was not permitted, and neither was *Forward Day by Day*. We were self-contained, like a congregational church.

In the summer of 2003, I watched and read reports of General Convention with great interest, but I spoke to no one about it. I had no Episcopal friends who shared my views—indeed my Episcopal experience in those days was a lonely one except for a friend who lived in the Diocese of California. When Gene Robinson received consents at General Convention, I celebrated by myself. But I knew this spelled trouble in my parish and my diocese.

It wasn't long before a meeting was called by Bishop Schofield. On that August Saturday in 2003, the cathedral was filled with clergy and laity from all parts of the diocese. The deputies from San Joaquin were seated at the front, facing everyone in the pews. The bishop, whom I'd only seen a few times, was seated in the front, looking formidable. I sat among several other members from St. Columba. I remember feeling anxious as I walked to my seat, and was greeted pleasantly by Michele Racusin, diaconal candidate at St. Columba. What I didn't know at that time is that Michele's call was to the priesthood. Under Bishop Schofield, there were no female priests in the Diocese of San Joaquin.

The deputies made their presentation, speaking only about Gene Robinson's appointment and condemning those who consented to it as willful children deliberately denying the word of God as revealed in scripture. One deputy told of looking at a painting of Jesus immediately after the vote, and seeing tears fall from his eyes. The bishop then opened the microphone for audience comments.

The line formed quickly. Clergy came forward first, all condemning the acts of The Episcopal Church. When one priest asked the bishop if we could remove our "Episcopal" signs, there was raucous applause and cries of assent: "Yes, remove our signs!" "We can no longer be called Episcopalians!" It reminded me of the crowd two thousand years ago who, whipped to frenzy, called out, "Crucify him!"

In response, the bishop, smiling and in control, urged patience. "No, not yet," he advised, magnanimously calming his flock, though he appeared pleased with the suggestion. "We must wait. I know it is difficult, my brothers and sisters, but the time is not yet."

I felt sick. As speaker after speaker took the microphone, I wanted to crawl out of my skin, slinking invisibly out of the pews into the bright sunshine. But instead I felt the collar of my shirt being tugged. I looked to see who it was, but only saw my fellow parishioners gazing intently at the speakers. My collar was pulled again, harder. There was no mistaking that I was being pulled from my seat, out of the pew and into the line for the microphone. I went.

I had no idea what to say—I felt too emotional, too powerless, too distressed. But I also felt clarity: I had to state my view, though it was contrary to that of every person in the large cathedral.

"Right Reverend Sir," I began, "I am Nancy Key of St. Columba Episcopal. I disagree with the other speakers. I am proud of what my church has done in electing Gene Robinson. I am not in favor of leaving The Episcopal Church." The cathedral was quiet.

"Thank you, Nancy. Thank you for stating your opinion," the bishop said with a note of sadness in his voice.

"It is important that all of us support those who have

different opinions," said one deputy kindly. I was later to learn that voice belonged to Father Rick Matters, a priest from Lodi.

As I walked back to my seat, a pin could have dropped like a cannonball in the cathedral. As I sat down, someone tapped me on the shoulder and said, "That was brave." Those words would be echoed by others after the meeting ended. No one, however, said, "I agree." I was, or so I thought, absolutely alone in my beliefs that the vote to consent to Gene's election was a holy vote, and that if the painting of Jesus were to come alive, it would be to come alive with joy and pleasure in the work of God's people.

The weeks after that day in August were quiet. My rector, Father Jim Snell, left a voice message inviting me to come to his office if I wanted to "chat." But the most important phone call was from Richard Jennings, a fellow parishioner I didn't know well. He told me he agreed with my statement at the diocesan meeting, and told me the history of our diocese and its long tradition of opposition to the wider Episcopal Church. There were others, he said, both laity and clergy, who shared my views, though none had come to the microphone that day. And, he added, Father Rick Matters, rector of St. John's in Lodi and the deputy who had responded to my comments at the microphone, wanted to talk with me. Father Rick, said Richard, believed as "we" did. This "we" was comforting—I'd thought, until Richard's call, that I was alone.

When Father Rick and I spoke on the phone, we decided that we must do something and began plans for a group we would call "Remain Episcopal." Rick knew there were others in the diocese who did not want to leave The Episcopal Church and who favored the consecration of Gene Robinson. With Rick's contacts, we put together a small meeting at my house. There were three clergy—Rick

Matters, Joel Miller, and Mark Hall—and several lay members.

Our small group became the executive committee of Remain Episcopal, and we met monthly. We set agendas, held butcher-paper planning discussions, and ultimately decided to form a 501(c)(3). (A 501(c)(3) for churches has specific requirements to maintain a tax-exempt status outlined by the IRS.) We wanted, more than anything, to educate the people of the diocese. Though we didn't think we could change the beliefs of the diocesan leadership, whose rhetoric became increasingly strident, we did believe in the "big tent" view of The Episcopal Church.

Our movement gained followers, especially in the northern and central parts of the diocese. We eventually had four clergy on our executive committee, and about twice that number of lay people. We elected officers—Rick and I jointly chaired the group, set agendas, kept minutes, and held monthly meetings. We also held regional meetings in Lodi/Stockton, Turlock, and Fresno. Eventually Cindy Smith and Jan Dunlap from Bakersfield would join us, as well as several members from Visalia, bringing in the southern part of the diocese. We identified our vision—to celebrate and proclaim the inclusive love of Jesus Christ in and through The Episcopal Church—and we set our goals. Working together, we would serve and protect those who wished to remain in The Episcopal Church, invite others into our community, and promote the ethos of The Episcopal Church.

Our principal tenet was to love those with whom we disagreed; schism was never our desire. Our strategy was to speak the truth with love. Perhaps we were naïve, but we persevered in this belief, probably much longer than was reasonable. We wanted to take the high road, rather than disrespect our bishop and those who believed differently than we did. But we were convinced that gay and lesbian people were full members of our body, and that their ministry should not be limited. While we understood the same gifts of women deserved honor, because Bishop Schofield made his main issue one of homosexuality, Remain Episcopal focused its work on the full inclusion of our gay and lesbian brothers and sisters.

Our band of intrepid believers continued to grow, and with our tax-exempt status we were able to accept donations. Most of the work was done by volunteers giving of their time and talents. In spring 2004, Rick and I flew to Atlanta to meet with twelve groups similar to ours springing up in other dioceses whose leadership opposed the Episcopal ethos. At the end of our three-day meetings, we had formed "Via Media USA," defining ourselves as a cooperative group whose purpose was to share support and information. We learned that the rhetoric and tactics used by leadership in each of our dioceses was similar, and we began to understand this movement toward schism as something far more deliberate and coordinated than it had appeared to us in our individual contexts. We were pleased that the Executive Council of The Episcopal Church sent two representatives, at our invitation, to this meeting. Though they explained that the church could not become involved in these activities in our dioceses, despite the clear signs that our leaders were headed toward schism, they let us know we had their unspoken support. With the first Via Media USA meeting, we worked even more strategically. We understood that we, in our individual dioceses, would need to be the voices of The Episcopal Church.

Remain Episcopal continued its work. We held regional meetings for people to share their stories, and we hosted informational gatherings around the dioceses. Pulling together mailing lists from as many congregations as we could, we sent out meeting announcements, which riled the clergy and drew the ire of the bishop at the 2004 Diocesan Convention. Our members made certain to attend all diocesan meetings to gather evidence. When Bishop Schofield shut down Trinity Mission in Madera—whose members wished to stay in The Episcopal Church—I called George Werner, then president of the House of Deputies, and sent pages of evidence to him and to David Beers, chancellor for the presiding bishop. George explained to me that they could do nothing—a fatal mistake, I thought, on the part of The Episcopal Church. They had essentially left us alone. While I realize that the Constitution and Canons made distinctions between the rights of a diocese and those of the wider church, even in those days there was plenty of evidence that the Diocese of San Joaquin was not adhering to those laws, at least in terms of its ban on the ordination of women to the priesthood. No one in The Episcopal Church dared intrude. No one dared recognize Remain Episcopal. Were we simply expendable?

At General Convention in 2006, Katharine Jefferts Schori was elected presiding bishop and Bonnie Anderson was elected president of the House of Deputies. These events gave Bishop Schofield the opportunity to intensify his attacks on The Episcopal Church. The members of Remain Episcopal were called unChristian, and individual priests attacked our members and the Remain Episcopal priests. One priest from Bishop Schofield's group called Holy Family Episcopal Church—which I had joined in 2004—a "den of vipers," and another pronounced Ichabod [1] on a Remain Episcopal priest. All the Remain Episcopal clergy were shunned at diocesan clergy meetings. At the 2006 Diocesan Convention, leaders fenced off the guest gallery with yellow police tape. That yellow tape became a metaphor of our

---

[1] "Ichabod" means the priest was "without glory."

separation from the diocese. But instead of being intimidated, we felt justified and unified. But most significantly, convention delegates voted to separate our diocese from The Episcopal Church. A constitutional change, this decision required two ballots one year apart to take effect. This was number one.

By this time, Remain Episcopal had gathered sufficient funds to hire an attorney, Michael Glass, who took on our case and who had worked pro bono since 2004. We increased our evidence gathering and continued our efforts. I spoke often in public, a far cry from my previous history of staying out of the line of fire. It was a curious thing: I felt certain, at all times, we must stand firm in our convictions that inclusion of all God's people was a sacramental necessity. I never questioned the truth of this belief, and I was not afraid. I was steeled by the prayer of St. Julian of Norwich:

> *All shall be well.*
> *All shall be well.*
> *And all manner of things shall be well.*

Each time there was a decision to be made, a view to be expressed, planning to be done, or comfort to be offered, my mouth opened and my feet moved. I feared nothing. I know now, as surely as I know my name, that God provided and the Holy Spirit gave me words when I needed to speak, strength when I needed to lead, love when I needed to comfort, and faith at all times. Just as I grew in the knowledge and love of Christ, it was evident that many of us in Remain Episcopal were similarly growing in our faith. It was a wonderful time!

Things changed wondrously for us in February 2007 when Bonnie Anderson came to the Diocese of San Joaquin, the first visit of any leader of The Episcopal Church in at least fifteen years. Since she was a layperson, she didn't need an invitation from the bishop, as clergy did, before coming to the diocese. Remain Episcopal organized a day-long event that began with a celebration of Eucharist at which Bonnie preached, a panel discussion, and lunch. Everyone—everyone!—was invited, including the bishop, who was seated in the front row with a number of clergy unfriendly to Remain Episcopal. It was a glorious day, and Bonnie made it clear that she supported our work and urged us to persevere. After the event she educated the Remain Episcopal leadership about Episcopal polity, making it clear that she would be always accessible to us. This was a turning point for us—we were no longer alone, separated from The Episcopal Church with whom we so much wanted unity. We had an important advocate. I know in my deepest heart that the Diocese of San Joaquin would not be a diocese today were it not for the Holy Spirit working through Bonnie Anderson. She is my hero.

In December 2007, the Diocese of San Joaquin voted at its Diocesan Convention to separate from The Episcopal Church: vote number two. None of us were surprised—this was a train on a one-way track. I suppose we were even a little relieved, for this meant we could turn our attention to rebuilding the Episcopal Diocese of San Joaquin. But we did feel a bit adrift between December 2007 and March 2008, the date of the special convention called by the presiding bishop. I spoke often with Bonnie, who advised me to "seize the vacuum." By this time Remain Episcopal was functioning as the leadership of the Episcopalians in our diocese, so vacuum-seizing was not foreign to any of us. We began working in earnest with the presiding bishop's staff on the next steps. It was an odd balance of power for us—in a sense I felt like we had been something like cowboys fending for ourselves in the wilderness, and now suddenly we needed to be both the local leaders and experts, and at the same time, hierarchy-respecters. Michael Glass helped immeasurably during this process.

We held our special convention in late March 2008, voting to elect Jerry Lamb as our provisional bishop in consultation with the presiding bishop. In the months and years since, our diocese has moved ahead, celebrating its inclusive policies, rejoicing in its growth, and impatiently awaiting the end of the legal battles. Our diocese has ordained several women to the priesthood, and Michele Racusin, who was kind to me at that diocesan meeting in 2003, was ordained a priest at Grace Cathedral, San Francisco, and is now rector of my church, Holy Family Episcopal in Fresno.

I have become more involved in my local parish, serving as eucharistic minister and visitor and lector. I am the chair of the San Joaquin Diocesan deputation to General Convention, and chair of the Standing Commission on Ministry Development for The Episcopal Church. The support of the larger church to the Diocese of San Joaquin remains a thrill. We feel loved and appreciated.

All manner of things shall be well.

Fresno, California
May 2011

Have Some Madera?

Richard Jennings

*Dr. Richard Jennings is a member of Diocesan Council and an ac-
tive parishioner of Holy Family Episcopal Church in Fresno. His
roots are deep in the Central Valley of California (Episcopal Diocese of San Joaquin), specifically in Madera and Fresno.*

In 2003 a group of Episcopalians in the Diocese of San Joaquin became concerned with threatening messages coming
from our then-bishop, John-David Schofield. We decided to
gather together for fellowship, and to educate one another on
what we learned and felt was happening in the diocese, and
what we could expect from The Episcopal Church. Organiza-
tional meetings were held every month at the home of Nancy
Key, and at my home too. Those Sunday-afternoon potlucks,
scheduled to last two hours, went on for four or more, as people expressed their concerns and frustrations. There were a
lot of tearful, soul-searching stories shared—and a lot of love
and respect given in return.

 I was born in Madera, California, into a family with
deep roots in the Central Valley, whose ancestors had settled

here in the 1850s and 1860s. There was little Episcopal presence in the rural cattle-raising areas, but my grandparents
were close to many families who were members of Trinity Episcopal Church, Madera, and St. Luke's Episcopal
Church, Merced. Our mutual relationships go back three
and four generations.

I have the advantage of seeing the Central Valley from
the eyes of one who lived in Southern California, attended
college there, and then returned to the Valley. When I did,
I shopped around for a spiritual home and found one in
The Episcopal Church. A second blessing is that at an early
age I figured out I was gay, and had no problem with that.
After all, my family had been here for five generations. The
important thing was family and preserving the mystique of
the land. No one in my family ever made an issue out of my
sexuality—how could they when there were so many divorc-
es, not to mention the uncles who did not marry and aunts
who could rope a steer and brand a cow? I was fortunate to
find a partner within three months of "coming out." I didn't
need to experiment or move to San Francisco to find someone, or live a certain lifestyle. Having made friends easily in
The Episcopal Church, I was able to develop talking relationships with straight as well as gay clergy and straight and
gay laypersons.

Bishop Victor Rivera (1968–1988)

In the late 1980s, our bishop, Victor Rivera, played an active
role in the selection of John-David Schofield as his successor.
The campaign leading up to the election of a bishop was the
first one I experienced, and I watched it, along with many
others, with interest. I can remember thinking, as did many
other Episcopalians, that Bishop Rivera was benign even
though he was very conservative, and a new bishop might

bring us into the mainstream of The Episcopal Church. We were concerned that Bishop Rivera had lost interest in supporting the provincial seminary, Church Divinity School of the Pacific, because he sent young men interested in the priesthood to Trinity in Ambridge, Pennsylvania, or Nashotah House in Wisconsin. We were puzzled that he didn't pay our diocese's full assessment to The Episcopal Church and troubled by his rejection of the ordination of women to the priesthood and his outspoken pronouncements on the issue of abortion. But we tolerated Bishop Rivera's old-fashioned ways because he was kind and we knew something better was to come.

There are many positive things to say about Bishop Rivera. I met him first when I was a representative on a diocesan mission commission. At one time this commission sponsored what was called World Missions Day at St. James Cathedral in Fresno. The fun, day-long event included panel discussions, fundraising sales, an inspirational talk from a missionary, and foods and entertainment from many cultures, with more than two hundred in attendance. When our Southeast Asian neighbors began to pour into the Central Valley, we were happy to reach out to them, and with the help of funding from The Episcopal Church, the diocese opened an Asian center that taught commercial sewing and English. At Holy Family Church we had more than forty Asian children in Sunday school. I didn't realize what a wonderful thing we had going here—until World Missions Day, without the support of the new bishop, was canceled.

Bishop Rivera and his wife, Barbara, were guests many times at our home for dinner. We had cordial discussions, and always just prior to leaving Bishop Rivera would say, "Next time Dr. Jennings, we need to talk about abortion." My response was always, "Okay," but that conversation never took place.

Bishop Rivera was a tireless builder of the diocese. He tried to open one new mission each year. Many of these missions did not survive, due to inadequate funding and poor oversight. He developed Camp San Joaquin as well as the Episcopal Camp and Conference Center (ECCO) in Oakhurst. I remember Bishop Rivera wearing jeans shoveling dirt at Camp San Joaquin. Although we did not see eye-to-eye on social issues, I learned to respect him and to look beyond his conservative ideals.

Bishop John-David Schofield (1988–2008)

But when Bishop Rivera retired, our new leader was a bull in a china shop: David Schofield. I had known of Bishop Schofield for years before his appointment to our diocese. Acquaintances remembered him from his days at St. Mary the Virgin in San Francisco, where he was a transitional deacon. A graduate of Dartmouth College and General Seminary, he had spent some time working in the East End of London. I once heard him talk about an experience there: While praying in a church, he had a vision of the Virgin Mary coming down from the stained glass window and reassuring him that everything would be all right.

The campaign for the new bishop of our diocese was interesting. We had an informational meeting at the cathedral to which many of the candidates were invited to meet with local Episcopalians. So many people turned out that the group was divided into five sessions, with each candidate giving a talk and answering questions. When Bishop Schofield entered our room, his first words were, "I want you to know three things: I am against abortion, I am against the ordination of women, and I am against the ordination of homosexuals." We were taken aback. That was a lot to throw out, especially when those three topics were not what most people expected to hear from a candidate. I did ask him a question regarding outreach, and his answer had something to do with a program in the Canal Area of San Rafael, just about an hour drive from his parish.

I did not support his candidacy. But he was elected on a Sunday afternoon at a special meeting in Visalia, after many delegates had gone home. The delegates from Holy Family reported the next Sunday on the election, and one woman broke into tears when she spoke of the tensions she felt in the meeting. She and her family subsequently left The Episcopal Church.

The first Diocesan Convention that Bishop Schofield chaired was in Hanford, and I was elected to a four-and-a-half-year term on the Diocesan Council. At that time, Council met on the third Wednesday of the month from ten in the morning until late afternoon, so working people had to give up one day of work a month. There were some great people on Council: a multimillionaire woman who made her fortune in construction, a funeral director, a pilot, and an assortment of "moderate" clergy. I was the youngest, the greenest, and the most naïve, and on most issues I kept my thoughts to myself. Little by little, I watched as lay members became disenchanted with the way things were going: Churches had begun losing members, income was down, and nothing was being done to address the issue. For the diocesan leadership, though, the solution was simple: They quit publishing figures.

Gradually the diocese paid less and less assessment to The Episcopal Church, not for lack of sufficient funds, but as a rejection of the Executive Council and General Convention decisions of the church. Eventually, the publication of *Forward Day by Day* was no longer available. As clergy retired or moved on, they were replaced by more conservative priests.

At every Council meeting we heard from the bishop of the theological and financial errors of "815." Never during my association with Bishop Schofield did I hear him speak favorably of The Episcopal Church, either its leaders or programs.

But throughout the years, I always tried to be on good terms with the bishop and his archdeacons—some five of them during the bishop's twenty-plus-year tenure. Every few months Bishop Schofield and I would run into each other at lunch and exchange cordial remarks. Up to the time of the schism, I thought I could be of value if I remained friendly with him.

Did all of this hurt my spiritual life? I think not. I firmly believe that all people are loved by God and called up to serve him. I do not think God has placed limits on what one is qualified to do or to be. If anything, Bishop Schofield made me think more about what I believed in and to be more outspoken. Did I feel abandoned by the church? No, I never did. The church, after all, is only the organization that humans have come up with to help explain what God is and what God has done. Throughout all of this, I believed more than ever that God does not abandon anyone. Remember the Good Shepherd who left his flock in search of one stray sheep? The shepherd could not abandon a sheep, and God could not, and will not, abandon any of us.

All meetings of Remain Episcopal were open to the public, and advertised as such; in fact, once Father Jim Snell of St. Columba tried to attend but went to the wrong home. I realized that the structure of our church limits the ability of outsiders to intervene with diocesan matters. Not everyone in Remain Episcopal, or the regular pew-sitter, understood that fact.

But all this stress did cause enormous frustration, especially as we at Remain Episcopal were often badmouthed by clergy and laity alike. It was frustrating to see the exodus of faithful parishioners from our church. Bishop Schofield and some of his clergy followers did great harm to the diocese and to the denomination by promoting a theology that few young people would or could relate to. As time went on, more and more people left The Episcopal Church in the Central Valley. The church, it seemed to them, was irrelevant to modern life. I can understand that feeling.

Loss of Spiritual Home Base

The greatest sin that occurred during the Schofield years was the closing of many parishes and missions and the subsequent selling of property and mishandling of trust funds. In many areas, families who for three or four generations had financially and emotionally supported their parish, had baptized their children there, had married and buried their parents and grandparents and great-grandparents there, found that their church no longer existed, separating them from their spiritual home and spiritual history. I don't have a number, but it is my guess that about ten churches or faith communities were closed. In many cases the closure came without notice or discussion. Many times, it was the archdeacon who acted as the "hatchet man," which separated the bishop from the action. After all, everyone believes that a bishop keeps the needs of his flock close to his heart and wouldn't close a church before trying every way to keep it open.

There's a story told about Bishop Kilmer Myers, bishop of the Diocese of California from 1966 to 1979. He was asked by a parishioner at All Saints' Episcopal in San Francisco's Haight-Ashbury district, in the 1960s when hippies were moving in and the families were fleeing to the suburbs, how many parishioners the parish would need to stay open. The bishop's response? Just three! Today All Saints' is a flourishing Anglo-Catholic parish. In the Diocese of San Joaquin, though, we suffered through dozens of closures—and all of them seemed to be done for the bishop's financial or punitive reasons.

The closure that I know most about is my home parish of Trinity, Madera. The church sat on three city lots in the oldest part of Madera, in an urban area that had transitioned to a barrio. The original brick structure was built in 1893 and enlarged later. In its 120 years of existence, the congregation played an active role in the spiritual and social life of Madera. Up until its closing, one of its ministries, St. Margaret's Guild, ran a thrift shop in the poorest part of town, where the church women and their friends worked together to meet the needs of the less fortunate.

Beginning in about 2004, we began to feel that things were not going well in Madera. Most of the congregation was unhappy with the priest, and had asked to talk with Bishop Schofield about it, but our request was denied. Months later, at a meeting at the bishop's office at the cathedral, forty people came to express their discontent. But they were told they would have to accept the current priest, and if not, the parish could always be closed and the "building bulldozed." The people returned to Madera dejected. Parishioners stopped attending and stopped their pledges, reasoning that if the church ran out of money, the priest would leave and they'd regroup and find someone else. But the diocese seemed to have other plans—the treasurer thought he could sell the land to a developer of multi-unit apartments. As it turned out, though, the church is in a historic district and the city would not issue permits for its destruction.

At the same time, there was so much tension in the churches in Fresno that an open deanery meeting was called at the cathedral, with Bishop Schofield officiating. He began by giving reasons why he felt the way he did and what he might do, then opened the meeting to questions. It wasn't long before prominent members of Trinity, Madera—a physician who was the third-generation parishioner, a retired school superintendent, a retired UCLA professor, and the mother of one of the city's biggest developers—began to ask about the status of their parish. After half an hour of questioning, an exasperated Bishop Schofield declared that "there are no Christians in Madera." There was a collective gasp from the 150 or so present. People stood, came to the microphone and scolded Bishop Schofield, and left. Those who had come to listen with an open mind and heart were leaving, discouraged and angry. I felt saddened at the spectacle of how hurtful people can be to one another—but satisfied that Bishop Schofield had finally "blown it" so publicly.

From its inception, Trinity, Madera had been spiritual home to many of the founding Madera County families. At the time of its closing, it could still claim as active members a couple of physicians, a dentist, a retired school superintendent, teachers, a lawyer, a judge, a couple of cowboys and farmers, the owner of the local paper, and a number of blue-collar folk. Many of these families had known each other for three generations, attending baptisms, weddings, and burials in the church and social events in the undercroft and garden.

The locking out of the congregation from the buildings, and the subsequent stripping of all things that could be sold or used by someone else, is difficult to understand. Everything was boxed and brought to Fresno where it was offered for sale. I was involved with the repurchase of three hundred-year-old Bibles, many hymnals, and other church memorabilia. Linens given in memory of a grandmother, books given to honor a grandfather, candleholders made by a parishioner—all were taken. Those not sold were to be "sent to Africa." The congregation was not informed of the sale; I happened to stumble on an announcement at a Diocesan Convention in Fresno.

One of my friends at Trinity, a fourth-generation parishioner and granddaughter of a long-time Sunday school teacher at Trinity, lamented that with the loss of the church there was no place to hold her grandmother's funeral service and so it was held at the graveside and the reception at a local restaurant. The grandmother had been the wife of the county veterinarian and a senior warden of the church. One of the Sunday school teacher's daughters worked in a local restaurant and for years buttonholed local farmers and businessmen to donate food for Christmas baskets that would be assembled in the undercroft of Trinity, but with the loss of Trinity, no more baskets were made. How many more people went hungry because of the sale?

The Trinity buildings were eventually sold for $385,000. What a tradeoff—the loss of a worshipping community's spiritual home, the loss of a thrift shop, the loss of Christmas baskets. Madera was poorer as it lost its witness of concern for the poor. That loss is sin. It also caused alienation of Episcopal Christians and negative feelings in the community. There is only a struggling Episcopal faith community in Madera today because the previous bishop and diocesan leadership absorbed all its resources.

In addition to closing churches, church schools were allowed to close or spin off as independent corporations. For four months I sat on the board of the day school at the cathedral. From what I understood, the school was doing fine and the parents had just had a big fundraiser to help with expenses. And then came a meeting at which the board was told the bishop and the vestry had decided to close the school. The buildings were offered to "New Creations Ministry," an evangelical group that works with homosexuals who are trying to become straight. The board members were shocked. Perhaps some members knew more than I did and didn't want to bring up issues at the monthly meetings.

Then there was the case of St. Clement's, Woodlake. In the late 1980s and early 1990s, the priest there was a man whose first career had been as a lawyer and whose first year on the Diocesan Council overlapped with my last year. Among St. Clement's parishioners was an extended family with three generations that called the church their spiritual home. One of the grandsons went off to college and came out as gay, and his partner was embraced by the entire family. Both young men came down with HIV/AIDS and the partner died. Though the young man's sexual orientation—or his illness—wasn't a secret at St Clement's, the priest began a series of sermons on the sin of homosexuality, implying inflammatory things about sexually transmitted diseases. One Sunday, as the priest continued to preach about these topics, the mother of the young man stood up and walked out. Two rows back another mother started to cry and ran out. The last time I spoke with the young man's mother she verified that she and her family, and other families, had not returned to St. Clement's since. I have no idea if this was an isolated incident, or if similar stories could be told of other churches in the diocese.

Joys

Enough of the sorrows and troubles. Christianity is not about dwelling on the negative: It is about the joy and promise of resurrection. Let me talk of the joys of being an Episcopalian in the reconstituted Episcopal Diocese of San Joaquin.

We know firsthand that we belong to a church that values all its members and appreciates their talents. We now have women in leadership positions among the clergy and laity. Gay clergy no longer must carry their secret. We have a transgendered person as well as an African-American man studying to be deacons at Church Divinity School of the Pacific. Look how far we've come!

We know that our church is willing to support us while we move beyond the schism. We've been blessed by the generosity of the Executive Council of The Episcopal Church, who have provided loans and grants, and we have received encouragement and support from Episcopal-related groups and foundations.

We can testify that God's hand is with us today, and that it will be with us tomorrow too. It may be years before the schism is resolved, and many more before congregations are reconciled. But we continue to give thanks to God for his loving care, and we go out into the world "to do the work that He has given us to do."

Fresno, California
May 2011

The Accidental Activist

Cindy Smith

Cindy J. Smith is president of the Standing Committee of the Diocese of San Joaquin and a member of St. Brigid's Episcopal Mission in Bakersfield. She is also a past president of Remain Episcopal and a delegate to General Convention 2012.

In 2002, I was received into The Episcopal Church in Bakersfield, California by Bishop John-David Schofield. The Episcopal Church was a perfect fit for me. I knew that because, like most new things I choose to do, I had researched it extensively. Jan, my partner of thirteen years, was a "cradle Episcopalian," having grown up in an Episcopal parish in New Jersey. As for me, I'd been raised in the Roman Catholic Church, attending Mass weekly with my parents until I left town for college, when I began my twenty-year hiatus from church—a common pattern for young adults. During those years, I returned home to Bakersfield, became a small business owner, and fell in love with Jan. When Jan decided to return to The Episcopal Church after a brief hiatus of her own, she encouraged me to attend with her. As for many who were raised Roman Catholic, it was a comfortable fit with familiar prayers and just the right amount of pageantry. My detailed research also presented a church that was liturgical and traditional, yet modern in its views on social justice, outreach, and—so important for my partner and me—the inclusion of all God's children.

What became more obvious with time was that The Episcopal Church in Bakersfield, in the Diocese of San Joaquin, was not the welcoming and inclusive Episcopal Church described in my research. There were good people in our congregation who were happy to see Cindy, and happy to see Jan, but many were not so happy about seeing Cindy *and* Jan. It became obvious that we were tolerated rather than accepted. We could participate up to point—as greeters, for example—but we should not expect to be involved in leadership or the governance of the congregation. I am a musician and was asked on a regular basis to perform instrumental solos and duets during worship, and whenever I did I could always count on one member of the choir to get up and walk out before my performance. It was an obvious statement that nobody stopped from happening.

I couldn't understand what had happened to "my" Episcopal Church—the church of acceptance and inclusion. Why wasn't it like that in Bakersfield? The "word on the street" was that *The* Episcopal Church—the national leadership—was misguided and heretical and that they'd lost their way. What I was hearing at the parish level just didn't make sense to me.

But in January of 2004, while working out of town on a multi-day project, I read a story in the local paper about a group of Episcopalians in the Diocese of San Joaquin—hey, that's *my* diocese!—who'd begun a grassroots effort called Remain Episcopal. The group defined themselves in positive terms, by what they were for rather than what they were against. To think I had to travel to San Luis Obispo, in the Diocese of El Camino Real, to find the true Episcopal Diocese of San Joaquin!

I contacted Nancy Key, the Remain Episcopal (RE) co-founder mentioned in the article, who invited Jan and me to Fresno for a meeting. We connected with a spirit-filled group that was glad to have us—both of us, together—as part of their extended community. In a little more than a year, Jan and I were invited to join the RE Steering Committee as representatives for the southern end of the valley. As we worked together with RE, several things became clear. The majority of the existing Episcopalians and congregations in San Joaquin were not aware of the real Episcopal Church. Their vision of the church was contorted; it had been molded by years of frightening falsehoods and by information that was controlled and filtered. There was little contact with the Episcopal world beyond our diocesan borders: no *Episcopal Life* publication, no word of the good work of Episcopal Relief & Development, no meaningful participation in General Convention. RE's vehicle for change became obvious—information. Get the real information to the people in the pews. With the availability of the Internet and search engines, the bishop's twenty-year-long control of communication could not continue. Via e-mail, websites, and blogs, the Internet would ultimately be critical to the success of the grassroots effort to continue the diocese within The Episcopal Church.

In 2006, Nancy Key encouraged me to be the next president of RE. I felt wholly unqualified for the task, but as we joke to this day, there is a handprint in the middle of my back that matches Nancy's hand exactly. Her gentle push and ongoing support allowed me not only to step into a new role of an "accidental activist," but has made me realize that

I will continue to express this passion for activism for the rest of my life. Shortly after taking the reins of RE, I began sending out weekly e-mail updates to our steering committee, concluding each note with a selected quote. The first one drew on the words of Gandhi: "Even if you are a minority of one, the truth is the truth."

By January of 2007, RE had been working to inform and support those faithful Episcopalians within the Diocese of San Joaquin for more than three years. Schism was imminent: The first vote to disaffiliate from The Episcopal Church had occurred, but a year would pass until the second vote would be taken. There were some voices in the blogosphere and other dioceses that were supportive of our cause but, for the most part, we felt alone. The leadership of Integrity USA, the Episcopal LGBT advocacy group, contacted RE, expressing an interest in holding their western leaders' conference in the diocese as a way to express their solidarity with those who had been oppressed and supporting our efforts to uphold the values and beliefs of The Episcopal Church. For me, this meeting was a life-changing event. Up close and personal, I had the opportunity to be with people who showed me you truly could be both Christian and gay—and that these identities were not mutually exclusive. From that experience came a comfort in my own skin that I'd never felt before. The meeting was also a Godsend for RE, as the good folks at Integrity gave us our first significant donation to continue our work, and provided input on upgrading our website to further our online efforts in spreading the word.

After the great morale booster of the Integrity visit, the long wait continued. The rational being in me understood why diocesan borders could not be crossed by bishops and why the powers-that-be had turned a (seemingly) deaf ear to our plight. But the emotional being felt only frustration and sorrow. If there was ever a time for a daring move to lift the spirits of the faithful Episcopalians, it was now. That move was made by Bonnie Anderson, president of the House of Deputies. As a layperson, she was able to cross diocesan borders and bring to us a message of hope and support from the wider church. At the time, it was a bold, even revolutionary, move. It is an excellent reminder to all laity that we too have a vital role in our church. Since 2007, Bonnie has continued this practice in other dioceses that struggle with issues of schism.

Also around this time, Jan and I made a second attempt to bring together an RE group in Bakersfield, our hometown in the southern end of the diocese. Twice, we rented a meeting room in the Beale Library and spread the word as best we could. We contacted several people who had written letters to the editor in the local paper after moving to town and being shocked by what they heard when they attended the local Episcopal church. Others had been here for some years, but had distanced themselves from the congregations as the misinformation was spread. From those meetings we formed a faith community that began to meet as a home church sharing a meal and Evening Prayer. We were blessed with an accomplished organist within our core group, whose portable keyboard provided wonderful music from the very first evening worship. Through the year as our numbers grew, we moved between homes. We adopted a "church in a box," transporting the worship essentials as needed. Perhaps most importantly, we learned just what *isn't* a necessity or essential for worship. Our travelling box of dining supplies earned the nickname "The Ark of the Condiments." We also planned for the future and met with representatives from First Congregational Church, the local United Church of Christ, and made arrangements to be allowed to use their small chapel at some undetermined time in the future, whenever schism might occur. Their caring and generosity toward us was amazing. Respecting the canons, our Bakersfield group held only Evening Prayer in the diocese until after the successful second disaffiliation vote was taken in December. Two weeks later, on Christmas Eve 2007, our first Bakersfield Eucharist was held in the borrowed chapel of FCC.

If we thought we had experienced the heights of frustration and inaction between the first and second schism votes, it was nothing compared to the limbo of the three months following the second vote in December 2007. The joy of finally having all the possibilities of embracing a true Episcopal ethos was tempered by the sadness of losing our church homes, the disappointment in friends who suddenly seemed to consider us as "others," and the realization that very, very little was left to work with—so few resources and people. We reached out to The Episcopal Church hierarchy to begin our rebuilding, but were surprised to find that what seemed crystal clear to us was murky from their perspective. To us the actions and words of Bishop Schofield were plain and distinct; he had left The Episcopal Church and formed a new diocese affiliated with the Southern Cone. But officially, canonically, and legally it was a quagmire. Was there still an ecclesiastical authority? Who owned church properties? Where would the small and dispersed faith communities find clergy support? For the next three months, we hung on as our leadership team worked through the many issues with our Episcopal Church contacts. Bonnie Anderson again appeared when we were in the greatest need. We held a celebratory worship service with the theme "Moving Forward, Welcoming All" in our beautiful hundred-year-old church in Hanford. With the strains of "All Are Welcome" rising to the rafters, for the first time in San Joaquin we saw women priests process and distribute Eucharist to

all present. It was a wonderful start to our new life as a diocese, shared via a live feed over the Internet to all our fellow Episcopalians. Two months later, we were fortunate to
have Bishop Jerry Lamb step forward and agree to postpone
his retirement (a second time!) to become our provisional
bishop. Then finally on March 29, 2008 in Lodi, with Presiding Bishop Katharine Jefferts Schori in attendance, we
held our special meeting of the Diocesan Convention and
Bishop Jerry was seated.

I was asked to be the chair of the nominations committee. The process was completed in eight days—all the
notice we had to put together the convention. In only eight
days, we sent out notices to as many of the Episcopal "rem-
nant" as we could find. We defined all the seats that had to
be filled, asked for nominations, sent informative descrip-
tions of the responsibilities of the offices (since few of the
remaining had ever held a delegate or diocesan position),
gathered bios and photos, and created a voter's guide. This
was critical, as very few members of one faith community
knew their fellow Episcopalians from other congregations.
Those who remained had not participated in what few diocesan events were held in the recent past. We were only
about one thousand Episcopalians spread over fourteen
counties in the middle third of California.

The entire eight-member Standing Committee was
elected that day. I was on the slate and received the long
four-year term as a result of receiving the most votes, probably due to my recent visibility as the president of RE. I
was surprised—did they realize I'd only been an Episcopalian for six years? After the convention, the new Standing
Committee met briefly to select officers and I was elected
as president. None of us—four clergy and four lay members—had any previous experience, but several members of
the Standing Committee from the neighboring Diocese of

California were there that day to help us "rookies" through the process of that first organizing meeting. They returned for a day some months later, for fellowship and discussion with our Standing Committee. This time they brought along members of their deputation, who conducted a training and orientation for the deputation of San Joaquin as we prepared as a diocese, for the first time in a very long time, to attend and fully participate in the General Convention of The Episcopal Church.

One of my most satisfying moments on the Standing Committee was authoring the resolution that created the Commission on Equality within the diocese. It was a unifying moment when the Standing Committee voted unanimously to sponsor the resolution and, before reaching the floor, more than a third of all congregations had signed on as co-sponsors and the resolution was passed in October 2008. The work of the Commission on Equality continues, most recently assisting the bishop in developing the guidelines and liturgy for same-gender blessings in the Diocese of San Joaquin.

RE continues with a focus on education of the Episcopal ethos and assistance to other dioceses facing schism. It supports faith communities as they host a series of workshops based on the Baptismal Covenant.

We have had many trials and tests over the last few years, but the people of the Episcopal Diocese of San Joaquin have stayed true to God's call and are a resurrection community. I have been so fortunate to have become an accidental activist in The Episcopal Church. Thanks be to God. Alleluia. Alleluia!

Bakersfield, California
June 2011

Rebirth of a Diocesan Office

Juanita Weber

Juanita Weber is a faithful member of St. Anne's Episcopal Church, Stockton. She became the San Joaquin Episcopal diocesan administrator in March 2003.

I moved from Pasadena to the Central Valley in 1978. I looked for an Episcopal church because The Episcopal Church I attended while I lived in the Los Angeles area had been important to me and my children, offering support, counseling, and a spiritual home during the years of my marriage and at the time of my divorce. My formation as a Christian had been started in a non-Pentecostal "holiness" church where my father was the pastor, but I really grew during my high school and college years as a participant in Young Life and InterVarsity Christian Fellowship.

My family and I were welcomed at St. Anne's in Stockton and immediately felt at home and became involved at many levels. I participated in the junior music camp at Camp San Joaquin, serving on the adult staff as my children attended first as campers, then as counselors as they grew older.

But it was at Camp San Joaquin in the 1990s that I began to notice that some people, especially from St. Anne's, were treated as "other." I met some of the clergy who had followed Bishop Schofield to San Joaquin when my children volunteered for staff in some of the other camps. I was appalled by their behavior and how they treated kids—labeling one young counselor as the influence of Satan; not eating with the kids at meals, but retreating to the cabin for a liquid (alcohol) meal; keeping kids at the chapel on the last night until way past ten when they made a confession of faith. I even witnessed these clergy members gathering for prayer to combat the "forces of evil" during an open meeting with the bishop to talk about women's ordination. It was also obvious at annual conventions when I attended as a delegate from St. Anne's that we were not accepted if we voted differently than the bishop expected. This was not the church I'd known back in Los Angeles.

It seemed that the best way to survive was to deal with the isolation from the rest of The Episcopal Church and the rest of the Diocese of San Joaquin and focus on the local congregation. I remember thinking when the rector who had been dean of the junior music camp left to move to another diocese, that it was not fair that the clergy could leave and find a job in a more compatible diocese, but that we laypeople were stuck because our jobs were here and we could not pick up and leave. When visiting churches in the Bay Area where my daughter was attending university, it felt really weird to be greeted with, "You poor thing," when the greeter found out I was from Stockton in the Diocese of San Joaquin. My daughter's response was, "But I am from St. Anne's—it's different there."

When St. Anne's called Mark Hall to be our rector,

Bishop Schofield held a lunch meeting with the wardens and the search committee. I asked to attend since I'd just been elected to the vestry. I was told not to come, but I crashed the meeting anyway. I listened as Bishop Schofield and the canon to the ordinary told us how bad Mark was. I had known Mark long enough to know that what they said was not true. Later the vestry investigated the bishop's claims, found them without merit, and called Mark anyway. Schofield did not contest our choice. He said that he gave in to us because the vote to call Mark was unanimous. I learned from those experiences not to trust what he said and not to trust those who bowed to him.

I was a delegate several times to the annual Diocesan Convention during the few years before the split. I remember the disconcerting feeling of having my name recorded when I voted; a secret ballot was denied. I remember people who I'd thought were my friends from other churches look right through me as if I didn't exist. It didn't feel good. But it did feel great to meet folks from other congregations who formed the Remain Episcopal organization. Their meetings often took place the evening after convention.

I retired from my day job as a consultant for the California School Age Families Education program with the California State Department of Education in February of 2008, soon after the vote to split and just before the special convention called by the presiding bishop. Mark Hall recruited me to help with the registration and logistics of the convention. I was glad to have something to do because although I was asked by the local child development community to get involved with the Local Child Care Planning Council and consult with teen parent programs in San Joaquin County, I really wanted to do something else. After the convention I held a meeting with the convention volunteers, wrote a report, and tried to turn in my key. I was told that

I couldn't leave—the reforming diocese needed me. That's when I started working in the diocese with Bishop Lamb and Canon Mark. I was glad that the skills I'd developed as a teacher, school administrator, and program consultant were needed. A few months later I wrote this for the *Friday Reflection*, our weekly diocesan e-newsletter:

> September has always been the start of the year for me. It was the beginning of the school year when I taught. Even when I worked as a consultant in the Department of Education, this time of year was a new beginning for the people in my program. Never in my wildest dreams did I think I would retire from a long career in education and find myself working in a diocesan office, researching policies and practices in the *Canons and Constitution of The Episcopal Church* instead of looking in the *Education Code*.
>
> One of my greatest joys has been getting to know so many of you by voice and e-mail. Hearing all of your stories, I have been able to share with you this new beginning in the Diocese of San Joaquin. What I do know is that God has a way of putting us in the right place at the right time, and as surely as I know that I can respond to His call to be here, answering your e-mail, I believe that He has called each of you to be where you are, from Ridgecrest to Lodi, to witness and be a part of this new beginning for San Joaquin.
>
> I have some vague memory of a Sunday school song from my childhood, "Jesus bids us shine—right in the corner, where you are," or something like that. So, for right now at least, this is my corner. Thanks be to God!

But first we needed a diocesan office. We had no resources except our faith and determination. The Executive Council of The Episcopal Church allowed us a practical line of credit so that we could rent office space, pay minimal salaries, and acquire office supplies. We had no personnel files as they were in Fresno with the deposed bishop. Fortunately, Canon Mark Hall had been in the diocese for a total of twenty-seven years. Because of this, he possessed invaluable information about the diocese and its history.

We rented office space from the United Church of Christ in Stockton and we bought secondhand office furniture and computers. It was a small space, with a tiny kitchen and three offices as well as a reception area—just right for our needs at that time.

Working for the diocese can be stressful, but it is life-giving and hopeful. I have seen folks throughout the diocese move beyond hurt and disillusionment to hope for the future. The process of regaining the Episcopal property is not completed, but being a part of and witnessing the rebirth of the diocese, as people find new avenues of outreach and service, has been exciting. Attending national conferences such as the Episcopal Business Administrator Conference, the Health Benefits Partnership Conference, and a lay CREDO where I experienced support from other diocesan staff and the Church Center personnel, has been affirming. We no longer are isolated from the rest of The Episcopal Church, and we do not need to isolate ourselves to be protected. This Episcopal Church is inclusive, affirming, and something I want to be a part of.

Modesto, California
March, 2011

By God's Grace

The Reverend Robert Woods

Father Robert D. M. "Bob" Woods is the current vicar of St. Sher-rian's in Kernville, California. A Scot with a bit of Welsh, English, and Alsatian, Bob immigrated to the United States with his parents in 1949. In 1951 the family moved to San Diego where Bob attended the University of San Diego, obtaining a law degree. After about a dozen years in legal practice, Bob felt an invisible hand on his shoulder, and was admitted to postulancy in the Diocese of San Diego. He attended Bloy House, the Episcopal School of Theology at Claremont, California, and was ordained to the deaconate in 1986 by Bishop Charles Brinkley Morton—also a reformed attorney. He first served at St. Dunstan's Episcopal Church in San Diego. Bob's legal career took him and his family to Bakersfield, where he was ordained priest in 1988 by Bishop Rivera. He served as interim and assistant at many churches in the Diocese of San Joaquin, and in 1998 became vicar of St. Peter's, Kernville, where he served until the schism. After being excluded from St. Peter's Anglican Church, Bob helped establish St. Sherrian's, Kernville. Now retired from law, he continues as a non-stipendiary priest.

I am a bi-vocational priest, so I've spent many years as supply, relief, and interim clergy all over the Diocese of San Joaquin. As a small-town mountain boy, I especially liked assignments in the Sierra Nevada. One such place was St. Peter's, Kernville, about sixty miles northeast of Bakersfield.

When I did a stint as interim in the late 1980s, my family and I would often drag our tent trailer up to Kernville for an idyllic weekend. St. Peter's had a checkered clergy history—a few priests had driven people away by the boatload—so I enjoyed assignments there regularly.

When I returned in 1996, I found a shrunken congregation with average attendance of eleven. I went twice a month and, slowly, people started returning. In 1998 I asked if, despite my day job, I could be their vicar, and my wish was granted. Within a year or two I discovered a couple of important things: First, that in a small community, word gets around and many previously disaffected parishioners returned and brought friends, and second, that Kernville would be a wonderful place to retire from secular work. St. Peter's was a good fit for my wife and me, and we and St. Peter's flourished, achieving over forty members on the books and an average attendance in the thirties. Indeed, such was the reputation of St. Peter's we actually had people attending regularly from as far away as Ridgecrest and Bakersfield, both some sixty miles distant.

Then came the election of the openly gay/partnered bishop in New Hampshire, and the beginning of polarization in the Diocese of San Joaquin. Growth, both in numbers and the Spirit, became stagnant. A handful of members with strong views managed to turn most coffee hours into polemical vociferation. Members began leaving after worship, and coffee hour became a "conservatives" club. Church membership and attendance slowly eroded.

Fast forward to just before 2006 and the first vote of the Diocese of San Joaquin to secede from The Episcopal Church. At our parish meeting, the majority at St. Peter's wished to stay in The Episcopal Church, no matter where they individually stood on the issues that were dividing us. Most understood that we have a big tent and that schism is a really bad thing. But when the diocesan vote went in favor of secession, St. Peter's became even more polarized. No more laughter at coffee hour and, worse, the level of mutual care, assistance, and cooperation among the congregation dropped markedly.

As vicar, I took fire from the more extreme proponents on either side of the issues. I strove, by appeal to scripture, early church fathers, and reason, to keep both sides focused on the core truth of our faith, emphasizing what we all shared and our duty to treat one another kindly. But my parishioners didn't seem to be listening. I was once called a "lame fence-sitter" based on my refusal to "make a clear statement" about the issues. My approach backfired, distancing the camps even further.

By 2007 and the final diocesan vote for secession, coffee hour consisted of two groups, like oil and water, occupying the same container but never, ever mixing. Came the parish meeting before the fateful Diocesan Convention, and air conditioning was no longer needed in the parish hall. I explained the larger issues—the Canons of Nicaea and what they said about church polity, the latent differences between the two sides on that and issues of biblical interpretation, eucharistic doctrine, and so on, noting that these matters were of greater importance than the gender and sexual issues. There was little discussion or interaction, and I decided on a private written parishioner vote as to secession, instead of a voice vote.

The results were not a surprise—eighteen to four in

favor of remaining with The Episcopal Church. We told our convention delegates and expected that they would vote accordingly at Diocesan Convention. But two circumstances kept that from happening.

First, the only people who were willing to serve as convention delegates (there was, among the "pro-TEC" people, some antipathy towards diocesan leadership) were "conservatives." Second, the morning of convention I awoke with a fever, and a look out the window revealed horizontal snow with no plants or asphalt in sight. I decided it wasn't worth the risk despite the issue, and I stayed home. So I wasn't there to shepherd our delegates, both of whom voted in favor of secession. One claimed ignorance of the outcome of the congregation's vote and the other indicated he "voted his conscience."

That was the last straw. Attendance plummeted and my every action and statement was subjected to questions and criticism. But I maintained my "Via Media" theology, which kept a dozen or so TEC supporters in our flock. I am a fan of the Oxford Movement and was raised in a "Faith and Order" environment, so bailing out on my bishop, no matter how wrong I might believe his position to be, was a very difficult step to take.

Former members asked me about starting an Episcopal Church congregation in the area, and asked how I could go along with the secessionist agenda. I explained that their "agenda" was not mine, but disobedience of my bishop was not an option so long as he was a bishop with jurisdiction within the Anglican Communion.

By chance, at about this time, I had met and spent an evening with somebody high up and well connected at Lambeth. Discussing the entire mess with this person, I discovered I'd misunderstood (or had been misinformed) about where the secessionist diocese and its bishop really stood. Some online checking confirmed that a diocese could elect a provisional bishop and that Bishop Lamb was now the real bishop. For me, that was that.

I printed out the information from the Anglican Communion website and presented it to the congregation, and asked if "we" should leave the "Anglican" Diocese and return to TEC. The majority, again, wished to be affiliated with The Episcopal Church. Amazingly, the very next Sunday there was an unannounced visit from Bishop Schofield's office, and I had the rare pleasure of proclaiming the Good News under the baleful stare of a diocesan representative, who later cloistered himself with the small conservative group.

Tension mounted and people kept leaving—my father and I represented almost two thirds of the church's income. Interestingly, I seemed to become a magnet for people who were disenchanted with the secessionist leadership—both locally and in the Province of the Southern Cone (consisting of Anglican churches in Argentina, Bolivia, Chile, Paraguay, Peru and Uruguay—and my pastoral care business flourished. In short, it was obvious St. Peter's could not live much longer in its current status, and that many souls were adrift, lacking a spiritual home and anchor.

Having done a bit of canon law while in San Diego, upon relocating to the Diocese of San Joaquin I was appointed church attorney and I continued in that role under Bishop Schofield. While it would be inappropriate for me to reveal advice given to Bishop Schofield, when I suggested that the diocese and its bishop were mistaken on certain issues of law and headed down a legally unsupportable road, my services were deemed no longer needed. That was a bit of a blessing, as serving in a remote mission church and being ignored by the diocese brought a little peace my way.

Even prior to the above events, I had spoken with Bishop Lamb about a seminarian who'd been under my tutelage in the pre-schismatic diocese. Bishop Lamb, in his kindness and acceptance, reminded me of Bishop Charles Brinkley Morton, who ordained me to the diaconate and who, like Bishop Lamb, was a consistent friend and spiritual resource. Bishop Lamb was kind enough to give me a few months to prepare St. Peter's for my departure from the Anglican Diocese of San Joaquin. I continued to emphasize the polity, comity, and overall theological issues, avoiding the "gay thing" in order to try to keep the parishioners engaged. Finally, when I was comfortable that everyone understood my thinking, I sent a letter to all members with a copy to Bishop Schofield and an accompanying letter to him, mailing it on a Friday with the intent of announcing my departure that Sunday. I offered to stay on until a replacement could be found, or to hold separate services, or provide the sacrament should they want a complete break, there being no Southern Cone priest within sixty miles of St. Peter's.

But on that very Sunday, I was treated to yet another unannounced visit from the diocese. I decided not to make my announcement at that time, but rather to talk to the diocesan representative after services and announce to the congregation the following Sunday—even though by then they'd already have my letter.

The response was immediate and, I feel, unfortunate. After revealing my intent, I was at first told "they hated to lose a good priest," that "they" understood my concerns, and that I should take a month or two to reconsider, since, after all, "they" were part of a "worldwide Anglican body," and so on. When I explained in detail my concerns based on my research and the apparent departure of the GAFCON (Global Anglican Futures Conference), a traditionalist group, departing from Anglican polity and norms of biblical interpretation, the diocesan representative made a phone call, then told me I was "relieved" from the position of vicar, that I was to remove my belongings within twenty-four hours and surrender my key immediately (they changed the locks the next day anyway). I was informed that I was not under any circumstances to perform any liturgical acts or provide pastoral services at St. Peter's or for its members.

I noted my willingness to stay on pending a replacement and to provide reserve sacrament or otherwise facilitate St. Peter's worship pending assignment of new clergy, but was told in forceful language that since I was no longer a "priest in good standing," my offer was unwanted. I admit to becoming a bit feisty myself, asking "their" theological and canonical basis for rejecting my priesthood—I was a priest of The Episcopal Church and therefore of the Anglican Communion. But I was told I just didn't understand.

A few weeks later the first service of St. Sherrian's Episcopal Mission, Kernville, took place with twelve of the remaining parishioners, leaving only six at St. Peter's Anglican. But more important than numbers, St. Sherrian's has become a happy, caring, accepting family as St. Peter's had been. Not everyone agrees on the all the issues, but we understand the importance of not further dismembering the Body of Christ.

In Advent 2010, St. Sherrian's moved from our former meeting place in the Kernville Oddfellows Hall, to Kernville United Methodist Church. There, we have joint services now and then, mingle over coffee, and support one another in word, actions, and prayer. We hope to establish an ELCA Lutheran presence too, since there are only two synodal Lutheran bodies here and a number of Lutherans without a church home.

The Kern River Valley is not affluent, and we remain

small and just marginally solvent. Yet, by God's grace we endure, by the Spirit we are filled with love and hope, and we celebrate the future for we know in whose hands the future rests.

Kernville, California
May 2011

If Only I Could Sing

Michelle Racusin

The Reverend Michelle Racusin is rector of Holy Family Episcopal Church in Fresno. A member of the Standing Committee, she is also a certified public accountant. She was one of the first women priests to be licensed by Bishop Lamb, on March 29, 2008.

What is a young girl to do when she wants to be active in a small conservative Episcopal parish and is too young to polish silver in the Altar Guild? She joins the junior choir and tries her best to sing. Desperate as the choir was for smiling faces, the only requirement was that these young girls process into the church reverently behind the cross carried by a boy acolyte and not fidget during the service. I could do that. Sing? Well, not so much.

During a choir practice break, I found myself inside the church asking God if it would be such a big deal to give me a beautiful voice. (After all, what is that to such a powerful God?) I was wandering up the aisles looking at the stained-glass windows when I saw the image of St. Barbara holding a chalice. I cannot explain it, but as I looked through that window, I knew—though I was just ten—that God was calling me to be a priest. When I turned to my best friend, who was standing beside me, and told her, she laughed and said, "That's stupid. Girls can't be priests." And she was right. It was 1968. The church didn't ordain women priests. But of course, the church didn't ordain children either. I would have to wait. God would work out the details.

I did not know how God would bring my ordination to fruition, but I was confident that he would. The years passed. The church canons changed and women were ordained. I graduated from college and graduate school and then obtained a professional credential as a CPA. At each juncture I asked God if it was time for me to start the process that would lead toward ordination. Each time I felt God say, "Wait." I married, and despite my friend's warning that I would never be ordained, we moved from the progressive Diocese of Los Angeles to the ultra-conservative Diocese of San Joaquin in the Central Valley of California. The move was a complete culture shock. San Joaquin had its own brand of The Episcopal Church, and I barely recognized it.

I went on to have four sons. God had said "wait" for so long, I reasoned that when they were out of college, perhaps then God would say: "Now." At that time, I'd probably move from the Valley to a place where God's call of women to the ordained ministry was obeyed. As I attended church in the diocese, I was amazed at how women, especially those who discerned a call to Holy Orders, were regarded as children of a lesser god.

But for the Grace of God

Yet God was not to be ridiculed as lesser because he called women to serve. In the quiet of an early morning more than three decades later, God said: "Now." My youngest son was three years old; I had a great career and a hefty mortgage; my husband had left his job in search of another closer to home. The wait had ended differently than I'd anticipated. But ... it had ended.

I went to the vicar of the mission I attended to explain that I felt called to the priesthood. After overcoming the shock that he was hearing this from a woman, he accompanied me to an appointment with the bishop, who in turn invited me to a discernment weekend hosted by the Bishop's Advisory Committee on Ministry. This dear priest, the vicar of the mission, was to be one of my strongest advocates.

The discernment weekend was filled with round-robin interviews with members of the Standing Committee and the Commission on Ministry, my husband and me, and other aspirants and their spouses. After one of the interviews, a priest threw my file on the table in front of me, ranting that I was not "born again." Another quipped that if I ever learned to preach, I'd be dangerous. Their mission, according to the bishop's wishes, was to reject me. Instead, by the grace of God, they reported back to the bishop that they had discerned in me a call to the priesthood. I'd later learn that the bishop was furious, but succumbing to pressure from a task force created by General Convention of The Episcopal Church to assist the four dioceses that hadn't yet ordained women, he acquiesced, reasoning that a woman with a demanding full-time career, four young children, and a Jewish husband would never survive the

additional rigors of seminary. It seemed a safe enough bet. I
was allowed to move forward.

My Grace Is Sufficient for You

Moving forward was by all human calculations unexpected.
But God wasn't hindered by misogynous frivolity. My academic experience was to be the easiest part of this grace-
filled venture.

I was to attend the local seminary that had just begun
as a joint venture between the Mennonite Brethren Church
and the Episcopal Diocese of San Joaquin, a partnership
intended to ensure that clergy raised up in the local diocese would not be exposed to the liberal, faltering, new-age
interpretation of scripture, or to the unorthodox direction
leaders believed The Episcopal Church was zealously pursuing. The professors, though, were very supportive. God's
grace abounded.

Even the bishop gave the appearance of support by
telling me that he would make sure I was ordained. The
dean of the Episcopal segment of the seminary repeatedly
assured me that the bishop would arrange to have another
bishop ordain women who concluded the process.

The academic side of school was a breeze for me,
though the schedule was grueling. I attended classes eve-
nings, weekends, and when my sixty-hour workweek as a
CPA with a large multinational firm was flexible enough, I
fit a class into the day. My circadian rhythm changed dra-
matically to accommodate work, school, and family. More
often than not I arose at 3:00 a.m. to study, read, and write
papers to reduce the impact on my family. Then I'd head
to work and class. My husband and sons were amazingly
supportive but I couldn't have done it without God's hand
in it. All said, I graduated in about three years—the same

timetable expected of someone going to seminary full time without a full-time job. I was the first graduate of this program.

The Silence of the Lamb

Had academics been the crux of this process, I'd have been home free. But of course academics didn't have a lot to do with it. The darkness of the Diocese of San Joaquin was unfathomable. It was abusive beyond imagination. The atmosphere was so treacherous that I felt like a lamb being led to slaughter. I kept my head in the grass and moved forward with stealth speed, determined not to fail. I remained silent.

The mission I'd attended for years—with the priest who'd been so supportive—closed and I was assigned to a large parish for formation as a seminarian. The rector, determined to purge me from the process, began his work. He was a master of isolating me from the parishioners. My presence as a seminarian was kept a virtual secret. When I wanted to teach a class, he allowed me, but when it was amazingly popular, he quashed my teaching another. I requested permission to teach at a Laotian mission connected to the parish and did so with his blessing, but was suddenly told not to return to complete the classes. And when one of the diocesan priests asked me to teach a class on the prophets for the school of deacons, as soon as the bishop heard, the rector made sure that I'd never teach at the diocesan level again.

I was never allowed to preach on a Sunday. Instead I was instructed to preach on three Thursday-morning services with an attendance of about seven parishioners. When I'd finished, the rector said I should never be allowed to preach. My seminary fieldwork supervisor found the rector to be so abusive that he wanted me to transfer to another supervisor. I begged him to ignore the abuse, fearing I'd be kicked out of the process for upsetting the applecart. When it came time for the vestry to move me forward in the ordination process, my paperwork was lost and it would be lost for months before it resurfaced.

There were incidents too numerous to name: the set-ups, the lack of support, the blindsiding. In fairness, it wasn't all at the hand of this rector—it was a carefully orchestrated plot. Financial aid had flowed to the men, not the women. My husband and I took on a second mortgage to pay for seminary. One of the diocesan staff had audited a class in which he had railed at me, calling me a "heretic" for pursuing Holy Orders.

Despite all this, I passed through the fire of my field training and seminary. When my graduation date came near, the rector inquired about the date and time—and did he need tickets to attend? Then he arranged to have the dedication of the new parish hall happen at the exact time and date of the graduation ceremony. So the bishop went to bless the building while the graduation ceremony at the seminary marking the first graduating Master of Divinity student with the joint venture between the Mennonite Seminary and the Episcopal Diocese of San Joaquin was snubbed. This was a great embarrassment at the seminary and I was to endure many disparaging comments from the seminary professors afterward.

Some seven months later, when the canonical exams were given by the local diocesan examining chaplains, rather than the General Ordination Exams, I was the only one in a field of several men to pass them.

With graduation and exams under my belt, and the task force from the General Convention of The Episcopal Church making inquiries regarding "assisting dioceses who had not yet ordained women," tensions at the diocesan level had heightened to a hysterical level.

My record had been stellar, but this would change. I had been invited to attend the ordination of a woman to the priesthood by a parishioner of the church I was serving. I'd known of this woman through my spiritual director and had corresponded with her occasionally. She'd been a member of the Diocese of San Joaquin but had transferred to a northern diocese to continue to ordination. When I told the rector about the ordination, he encouraged me to go, and the following Sunday he inquired about the event. I told him about the ceremony with stifled enthusiasm. The following day he reported to the bishop that I'd attended the ordination, and before I knew it I was summoned to the bishop for a "grave concern." How could I have been so naive?

I went to the diocesan house and waited as the rector and the bishop met. When I was called into the office to meet both of them, I observed a stack of my Ember Day letters (seminarians' letters to their bishop) sitting on the bishop's desk. The bishop began by stating that in evaluating me he was concerned on a number of points. One, that I was "unevenly yoked." My husband was Jewish, he said, which would present an untenable situation for my ministry. Two, he hinted that my husband's conversion and baptism may have been a ruse to help his wife in the ordination process. Such a ruse, he said, meant that a millstone should be tied around my neck and that I should be drowned in the deepest of rivers. Three, he said that I was not a Christian because I had attended a woman's ordination. And four, because my Ember Day letters were so wonderful, rather than purge me from the process, he would transfer me to another parish for rehabilitation.

I went on to this parish to be reformed and to await my ordination to the diaconate. I remember my first Sunday there. As I vested in a library, I looked at the books lining the walls and saw several shelves dedicated to treatises arguing against the ordination of women. I was amazed at the wasted energy. Yet I remained silent.

By now the General Convention's affirmation of the selection of an openly gay and partnered bishop had given the bishop of San Joaquin new energy. While he knew that he would no longer be able to garner sufficient support in the diocese to separate from The Episcopal Church based on women's ordination, he knew he stood a chance by convincing people that the church had misinterpreted scripture with respect to gays and the time had come for San Joaquin to stand up for orthodoxy. It was in this climate that he no longer felt any need to feign compliance to the greater church on women's ordination.

It was in this atmosphere that the bishop made me a deacon and promised that after one year I could pursue the priesthood. Again, no one expected that I, with my full-time career and my family, would realistically move forward. I was still a safe bet. I was obedient and I was silent.

You May Go . . . But . . .

After one year, I went to the bishop to request release to another diocese to pursue ordination to the priesthood. I sensed a great deal of relief on his part. He named three surrounding dioceses that he would release me to: Northern California, San Diego, or Rio Grande only. All others were non-Christian. Out of obedience, I chose one of the three he selected. After a brief meeting with the bishop of that diocese, I requested to be canonically transferred.

It was not to be. The bishop of that other diocese said, "No."

The Swing Vote

There were many who preached that women should not be ordained. My belief has always been that I would rather face judgment in which Christ demanded of me, "Why did you over-preach the Gospel, woman?" than to face the disappointment of God who said, "You knew I called you; why did you succumb to the influence of deceivers?"

So I marched on; on to the Diocese of California. Not on the bishop's list, but now all bets were off.

Bishop Swing listened to me and agreed to move me forward in the process in the Diocese of California. In June 2005, close to four decades after God had called me to the priesthood through that stained-glass window of St. Barbara in my childhood parish, I was ordained a priest in God's one holy catholic and apostolic Church.

On that day I could sing.

Already—Not Yet

I was to work at Grace Cathedral, the place of my ordination, for a little over three years. Holding on to my accounting career and commuting some three hours and forty-five minutes each way, I traveled to the city each Sunday to celebrate the Eucharist at the cathedral. It was a glorious time for me as I began to learn what it meant to live into the priesthood. On each Sunday morning, I would arouse one of my sleepy sons who would travel with me to the cathedral and back. It was some of the most precious time I ever spent with my children and it was a gift that I could never have expected.

In the midst of this, the Diocese of San Joaquin attempted to separate from the The Episcopal Church. I was in a big box store at the time of the vote. When my priest friend, who had been my support from the very beginning, called me on my cell phone to report the vote, my eyes swelled with tears. One of my sons looked at me and in astonishment said, "You expected this—why the tears?" I really didn't know. It seemed so wrong, so violent. It was a death. Yet with every death comes resurrection.

A special convention would follow as the diocese rebirthed and Jerry Lamb was elected provisional bishop. In his first act of convention, he licensed four women priests. I was among them. The delegates were elated. A sense of belonging to the wider church had begun.

Yet I didn't believe that God would call me to full-time ministry. I'd figure that out later. But when I did, it was Bishop Lamb who helped me discern how that call would manifest itself in the resurrected diocese.

And—go figure—it started in the parish in Fresno where my family attended while I served at the cathedral in San Francisco. It was in that church in Fresno that I became the first woman rector in the diocese.

Singing a New Song

If I could have sung a lilting hymn at age ten, my life perhaps would be different. But I could not. Yet God takes our voices and uses them for his purpose. I was called to a peculiar ministry through a stained-glass window at an early age by God who does not regard women as inferior. I was placed in the Diocese of San Joaquin for his purpose. Together, with many others, we are singing a new song. It is the song of Resurrection.

Fresno, California
May 2011

New Light Brings New Life

Suzy Ward

In 2009 Suzy Ward was the first woman ordained to the priesthood in the Episcopal Diocese of San Joaquin. She remained as a deacon in the diocese for twelve years waiting for the right time to follow her calling to the priesthood. She now serves as the priest-in-charge of an Episcopal congregation that remained when the other members of the congregation voted to follow John-David Schofield out of The Episcopal Church. Suzy also serves as a full-time kindergarten teacher for Tulare City Schools.

It was one of those beautiful San Francisco days: the sky clear and blue; the temperature a perfect seventy degrees. As I drove to Grace Cathedral, I was nervous about wearing my clericals. I was a stranger, an outsider. But I was there to celebrate with my friend Michelle, the first woman I'd see ordained to the priesthood. The only female priest I knew was Nedi Rivera and she was a bishop now. But now I would know Michelle. How long I'd waited to see this. We had been in seminary together. She'd been the brave one who'd found a way out. I was still waiting.

I arrived early, with a whole hour to wait. I parked and decided a cup of tea would be good and I could read in the courtyard. As I walked around there were others who'd come early, families and friends of the ordinands, I assumed. I went down the steps into the basement where they sold coffee and tea, and that was when I noticed it. There were all these other women with funny collars. Women clergy were everywhere in this place. They were sitting at tables, talking, laughing, and just enjoying being together.

I went to the courtyard to sit and write in my journal. All I could think of was how much light there seemed to be around me. Though it was a glorious, sunny San Francisco morning, there seemed to be an aura of light that wasn't just about weather. It was like the light that fills a room after the drapes have been pulled back. The radiance of the sunlight filled the space. There was no darkness here.

Even within the sanctuary of the cathedral, the subdued light was tinted by the brilliant colors of the stained-glass windows. The light this day seemed to be unique, somehow different—brighter, warmer, more filled with a living presence.

The ordination service began, followed by the Eucharist, with all these newly ordained clergy assisting. Finally I knelt for my first blessing by my friend who was now a priest, and received her sacramental blessing. This truly was a different place, a place of new life, new experiences, and new light. I felt safe here.

My faith, my hope, was enlivened in a way that I had never experienced before. My spirit soared in praise. "Praise be to the God and Father of our Lord Jesus Christ! In his great mercy he has given us new birth into a living hope through the resurrection of Jesus Christ from the dead, and into an inheritance that can never perish, spoil or fade—

kept in heaven for you, who through faith are shielded by God's power until the coming of the salvation that is ready to be revealed in the last time." (1 Peter: 3–5)

There was a new hope in my heart. There was nothing that could spoil or fade the new ministry that had been given to Michelle that day. But then I thought of my own ministry, my own path. Where was the hope and light for me? These thoughts haunted me as I drove back to the Valley. The further away from San Francisco I drove, the more the new sense of joy and life that I'd felt seemed to be ebbing away. When I got home and tried to explain to family and friends about the wonderful light that I had experienced, the only metaphor I could adequately produce was that of being a time traveler. I'd had an opportunity to experience life in the Age of Reason, the Renaissance, and now I'd returned to the Dark Ages, a time when the world hid in fear and superstition. I wondered if I'd ever experience that hope, new light, and new life again? Through the struggles and darkness I knew in my heart that my faith was being tempered and strengthened. "In this you greatly rejoice, though now for a little while you may have had to suffer grief in all kinds of trials. These have come so that your faith—of greater worth than gold, which perishes even though refined by fire—may be proved genuine and may result in praise, glory and honor when Jesus Christ is revealed." (1 Peter: 6–7)

My time did come. It took a while. It took patience, undaunted determination, and support and love from many places and many people. The greatest deterrent was the diocese itself. There was no evidence that a model of shepherding people through a process of discernment to ordination was ever considered. For me it had become something I tried to avoid. I'd already been ordained a deacon. Why wasn't that enough? Yet my heart, my very spirit, told me that I was being called to the priesthood. But why go through that process again? It was all about the questions they would ask and the superior attitude they held over me. Their questions weren't about helping me peel back the layers of faith, to discern at a deeper level how God was calling me to a new ministry. No, these were questions that seemed to be aimed at tripping me up, making me say something that would indicate that I wasn't a true believer or worthy of being allowed into their brotherhood. They questioned the fact that my husband didn't attend church, calling us unequally yoked. They asked me about Gene Robinson's election as bishop. Then there was the day they asked me to define "truth" in a twenty-minute interview. That was the day I knew that they were looking for something other than my call. But the Spirit of God that lived within me kept whispering to me, words from a song that I love, "For such a time as this I was placed upon this earth to hear the voice of God and do his will." I couldn't have stopped if I'd wanted to. God is pushy that way.

But at each meeting of the Commission on Ministry, I received the go-ahead. Someone was helping me out. But there would come a point when I needed to become a candidate and so I purposely bided my time, as I wanted to be ordained in the Diocese of San Joaquin. I was repeatedly asked but I repeatedly said no, not yet. My own priest knew I was stalling. But I didn't want to get trapped by a canonical requirement that would stop me from being ordained in this diocese. Graduation from seminary was still a couple of years away. I was on the turtle track. So I waited. Patience is a smart move when it can save you from going headlong into a battle that you can't possibly win. I knew in this place and at this time I would never win, so I waited.

As I waited, the darkness of the diocese became even more troubling. The Diocesan Convention of 2007 opened a floodgate of emotions and accusations that tore at the very fabric of not only my faith but that of many in the diocese. In the early days after the first vote in 2006, I wondered where the vote would take not only me but my church home and family. But the rhetoric and anger from the pulpit soon led me to understand that there had been such a tear in the fabric that it was beyond repair. There was backroom drama; there was frustration, confusion, and questions—but no answers. It was a time of great uncertainty for those who were left outside, with no power to make decisions.

At my parish many looked to me for answers but I felt as out of touch and powerless as they were. I tried to stay focused on my classes. But the time came and the rector and vestry said a vote had to be taken, a vote that would change the life of this beautiful brick church forever. In the weeks before the vote, the leaders thought that both sides should be represented. I was the only clergy person who stood for The Episcopal Church in my parish so I and a couple of others were asked to be the panel to present the arguments for why we should stay within the structure of The Episcopal Church. The other side included the power brokers of the church and, though he was supposed remain on the sidelines, the rector himself.

Three Sundays in a row we debated and then the parish voted. We had hoped for more, but it is scary how fear and the cult of a personality can impel highly educated people to follow. The vote was about changing the parish bylaws, removing any association to The Episcopal Church, but it was really a declaration that said, "We are leaving." It was only a few weeks until Easter. How could we celebrate new life, a resurrected life in such a setting?

I gave my notice to the rector, explaining that my last Sunday would be Easter. I had trouble saying those words: "my last Sunday." What was to happen next? Where would

I serve as a deacon again? I knew that a handful of parishioners would stay together but how would it all come together?

My last Sunday in this beautiful building was supposed to be a day celebrating the resurrection of Jesus Christ. For me it was a day of deep sorrow and sadness as I quietly removed my few stoles from the sacristy. I served at three services that day. Each time as I gazed at the cross hanging in the narthex I felt the sorrow begin to climb to the surface and I would have to say a prayer to control the feelings and the tears that lay right at the jagged edge of my emotions. It was easily the worst Easter I hope I ever have to experience. At one moment between services, I tried to slip quietly into the church to experience one last time its comforting silence, to experience the new light of Easter through the windows that told the story of the great paschal mystery, the sacrifice of the lamb and the tomb that could not hold our Savior. But there he was—the rector. I sat down, hoping to avoid too much conversation. He spoke quietly, "I think I understand how hard this must be for you." I don't remember what I said or what he might have said next, but maybe for the first and only time in our twenty-year relationship did I feel he understood me. When the last service of the day was over, without speaking to anyone, I quietly slipped out the door with my robes on my arm and walked to my car. I could hardly drive home.

The next Sunday and for many Sundays after that painful Easter, I found a place and people to worship with and to faithfully serve as a deacon. This ongoing Episcopal congregation met in a school cafeteria with the hum of a soda machine in the background. We carried in boxes of books, set up an altar, and brought in a keyboard. Every Sunday we packed and unpacked our "church in a box." There was even a Sunday when whatever permission we needed wasn't obtained and we gathered around the concrete tables on the playground. But we were a community of people who loved the Lord and we were thankful to be together. People looked to me to keep them together—though a deacon still, I was considered the leader. Always my thought was how to create a community where everyone had a voice, where no one was a stranger or a power broker. There were only to be servants and missionaries who went into the world each Sunday rejoicing in the power of the Spirit, looking for opportunities to love and serve the Lord. The light that I'd experienced that day in San Francisco was breaking through right here in this small community of faithful Episcopalians who worshipped in school cafeterias and playgrounds.

In ways many of us had never experienced before, we were truly living out the faith we'd accepted at our baptism. "Though you have not seen him, you love him; and even though you do not see him now, you believe in him and are filled with an inexpressible and glorious joy, for you are receiving the goal of your faith, the salvation of your soul." (1 Peter: 8–9)

After all the waiting, after all the classes, exams, and appearances before committees, the day came for my ordination to the priesthood. Bishop Nedi Rivera was the preacher and Bishop Jerry Lamb the celebrant. Between the two I don't know who was the happiest that this day had finally come for this diocese. For the story was no longer just my story; it was the story of the diocese. It was the story of the new light that had come into San Joaquin for everyone to experience. We were building a house where all were truly welcomed. The hymn we sang that day was the story of the new diocese that was being reborn. All are welcome!

As Episcopalians we believe that all are called to ministry. That day was a celebration and an affirmation that in this diocese these words that all are welcome were true, that there were no boundaries or barriers to the fulfillment of our calling to serve God in whatever order of ministry we are called to serve.

In our baptism we are reborn to new life in Christ. Our baptism is like the living coals from the fire on the altar from which the seraphs touched Isaiah's lips in a dream, blotting out his sins. Our sins had been blotted out; our old life had been put aside. We had experienced death. Now we were experiencing resurrection. As Bishop Nedi said in her sermon that day, "This is a Big Deal Day!" The barriers and blockades had been pulled down and the doors of the church were opened welcoming all, and they would never be closed again. Paraphrasing Nedi's sermon, "The long winter of our struggle is over. There is new life. We are not being resuscitated back to life, but to a new life—a new life that has never been seen before." It wasn't about me and my ordination, Nedi insisted, because that June day in Hanford was about the church and the people who are the church. God calls and asks, "Whom shall I send?" With the freedom found in the new life of resurrection, we can all now say, "Here am I; send me."

Visalia, California
May 2011

A Farcical Candidacy

Kathryn Galicia

The Reverend Kathryn Galicia, priest-in-charge of St. Francis Episcopal Mission, is vice-chair of the Commission on Ministry and chair of the Examining Chaplains in the Episcopal Diocese of San Joaquin. She is employed part time at Orchard Supply Hardware. The following is her struggle to fulfill her call to ministry.

I am a cradle Episcopalian who grew up in a family where church was important and our lives were centered around parish ministries. Like many people who came of age in the 1960s and 1970s, though, I drifted away from church activities after leaving high school, and later, when I moved to California, I didn't look for a church in my new home. But I continued to attend church with my parents whenever I went to visit them.

I met my husband, Al, at the University of California at Santa Barbara. We were married in 1979, and his career as a retail store manager led us to many different places—in the early days of our marriage, we moved seven times in six years. A few years before our son Christopher was born in 1988, we settled in Pleasanton, where we remained for about ten years. When Chris was just starting kindergarten, Al was transferred to Modesto, where we bought the house in which we still live.

When Chris was a toddler, we began attending St. Clare's Episcopal Church in Pleasanton, but didn't get involved in any of the ministries there. I was attracted to the choir, but between working full time, having a family, and attending school, I just couldn't find the time.

A major shift in my spiritual life happened not long after we moved to Modesto. I hadn't gone to church at all since our move, as my retail job required me to work on most Sundays. But in 1995, my mother passed away, and after I returned from her memorial service in my hometown, I felt a strong pull back to the church. I asked my employer for a schedule change, then phoned the closest Episcopal Church, St. Dunstan's, but was disappointed to get only an answering machine. But a couple of days later, I received a hand-written card from the vicar, the Reverend Duane Peterson, who wrote that they were looking forward to our first visit on Sunday. As it turned out, Father Duane had only been there a couple of weeks himself, and was just settling in. His wife, Mindy, was teaching Sunday School, where Chris was welcomed with open arms. After attending the 10:00 a.m. Sunday service for a few weeks, I couldn't help noticing that the choir was very small, and not very enthusiastic, though the organist was quite good. At coffee hour, I approached one of the choir members and, somewhat hesitatingly, asked her if there was a chance I might be allowed to join. Her response? "Oh, honey!" and a big hug. I wasn't even asked if I could sing! I became a regular choir member, which gave me a reason to go to church every Sunday, and to attend a weekly choir rehearsal when my school and work schedule allowed.

Thus began my ministry in The Episcopal Church. Soon, I was asked to become a licensed lay reader, which entailed going to lay ministry conferences in Manteca and Hanford. As I learned about and practiced each new ministry to which God called me, I felt that I was on a path leading me ever more deeply into relationship with Jesus. Two of the ladies from the choir had started a ministry to a local nursing home and invited me to join them. Each Thursday, they'd visit the home and do a brief Morning Prayer service along with music—mostly old gospel hymns, not many of which were in our 1982 Hymnal. Perhaps because my father was living in a nursing home in Buffalo, I felt called to help bring the love of Christ to the residents in Modesto. Over the next couple of years, I learned a lot of new spiritual songs and was blessed with getting to know the residents. Sometimes I brought my guitar, but mostly we sang along with our enthusiastic pianist.

Around the beginning of 1997, Father Duane talked with me about the possibility of becoming a deacon in the church. I knew very little about deacons—I had no idea what deacons did or what the training process would require. Father Duane explained diaconal ministry to me, and added that the educational requirements would include a three-year program in Fresno. I learned that in the Diocese of San Joaquin, under the leadership of Bishop John-David Schofield, though women couldn't be ordained to the priesthood, they could become deacons. I was shocked. The priest who had conducted my mother's memorial service, in the very church I had attended during high school, was a woman. My parents loved her and her gender had never been a problem. I also knew that there had been women priests around the East Bay area. So the fact that our bishop didn't "allow" women to be priests really bothered me. I politely told Father

Duane that the process of becoming a deacon wasn't possible for me, with my commitments to my family and job. I was also planning to go back to college to finish my B.A. and elementary teaching credential. Though I was pleased that my parish had recognized in me a call to ordained ministry, it all sounded too complicated. As a woman, knowing that the diaconate was the only option open to me really upset my sense of justice.

There's a cliché that "when God closes a door, God opens a window." I think it's also true that when we say "no" to God, God just finds another way to reach us. In my case, it was through music. I loved singing in the choir, and it literally helped me find my voice. Our organist and choir director at St. Dunstan's graduated from high school and was ready to move out of state for college, and another young man took his place, but only for a few weeks. One Sunday morning, Father Duane spoke to me after church, asking if I might play the organ until they could find a regular organist. My first inclination was to decline, knowing that I wasn't very good at the piano, let alone the organ. But the evening before, while visiting a neighbor, I'd remarked on the nice electronic organ in her family room—and Janna, explaining that she wanted to get rid of it, offered it to me. The organ was happily accepted, and we moved it across the street that very night. And the next day, Father Duane asked if I would be willing to play. It seemed as though I really was expected to say yes.

Soon I was taking organ lessons at the junior college, and doing a reasonable job at holding the choir together and playing for Sunday's 10:00 a.m. service. That led to more musical discoveries as other members joined, including some talented people who formed a small group to do anthems and other special music. As I grew more involved in leading the music at church, I enjoyed it more and my confidence grew. I was able to play for weddings and funerals, and my knowledge of liturgy and music within The Episcopal Church grew. Around that time I was also elected to serve on the bishop's committee, which gave me additional knowledge and experience in what church was all about.

Father Duane surprised us all in 1998 when he announced that he had accepted a position in Louisiana, and left soon after. Looking back on it now, I believe that he sensed the fight that was coming in our diocese and made the decision not to be a part of it. He was a very good pastor but didn't like conflict. He made the right decision. I was on the search committee to help find a new vicar, but there weren't many choices. We had a strong lay leadership group, but St. Dunstan's had gained a reputation as a "difficult" parish, and the average tenure for a priest at that church was about two years. In the forty years since its founding as a mission from St. Paul's in Modesto, St. Dunstan's was unable to be self-supporting. It remained a mission church, although it had an average Sunday attendance of around eighty at that time.

Bishop Schofield sent his canon to the ordinary, Jim Thompson, to help direct our search, and they appointed an interim priest, the Reverend Malcolm McClenaghan, to lead worship services and to act as our advisor during the search. I enjoyed "Father Mac," and learned a lot from his between-services adult studies and his excellent advice on stewardship. The main problem was that he lived about twenty miles north of Sacramento and could only be with us on Sundays. He was retired, and was also actively involved in developing low-cost housing for the elderly, which involved some traveling.

After a lengthy search process, one candidate for vicar showed some interest, and we jumped at the chance to interview him. Canon Jim Thompson called a meeting of the search committee and anyone else who wished to attend, where he introduced us to the Reverend Anthony Morello, from the Diocese of Los Angeles. Father Morello explained why he had to leave his last post, and told of his experience in ministry over the previous decade or so. Both Bishop Schofield and Canon Thompson, in a meeting that followed this introduction, urged us to accept Father Morello as our new vicar. The reality was that if we declined, no one else was likely to apply in the near future. Some felt that waiting for another candidate would result in losing more members as people drifted away to other parishes with permanent clergy. We made the decision to call Father Morello as the new vicar of St. Dunstan's. A dynamic preacher and excellent storyteller, Father Tony made a great impression on nearly everyone, and some of our lapsed members returned at the beginning of his tenure.

Meanwhile, after being accepted in the process leading to ordained ministry, I began taking classes at the Mennonite Brethren Biblical Seminary, attached to Fresno Pacific University. At first, I took the nine core Anglican Studies classes, which were offered on weekends. These were administered in a partnership between the Mennonite Seminary, the diocese's San Joaquin School for Ministry, and Trinity Episcopal Seminary, in Ambridge, Pennsylvania. Some of our teachers were adjunct professors from Trinity; some were local priests from our own diocese. During this period, I was also completing my bachelor's degree in social science from Chapman University, and I continued to work full time at Orchard Supply Hardware.

My seminary options with Bishop Schofield were few. He allowed people to attend Nashotah House in Wisconsin, Trinity in Ambridge, or the Mennonite Seminary in Fresno. Someone told me that under no circumstances was I even to utter "CDSP" (Church Divinity School of the Pacific), under threat of being cast out of his office. Though that was where I wanted to go, I bit my tongue. I was attracted to the Anglo-Catholic theology of Nashotah House, until I read in their catalog that out of concern for people's feelings, women priests were not allowed to celebrate at the altar. (That policy, I understand, has since been changed.) After discussing the possibility with my family of living in a cold climate for the next three years, I elected to do my Master of Divinity in Fresno. It turned out to be the best choice under the circumstances.

At the beginning of the ordination process, the prohibition against the ordination of women as priests didn't seem to be a huge roadblock. At General Convention in 2000, the bishops of the dioceses not ordaining women were mandated to do so by 2004. It seemed as though I had the wonderful blessing of falling into that brief window of time in which becoming a priest in San Joaquin was possible. At a meeting with Bishop Schofield early in 2001, he assured me that, although he wouldn't personally do the ordination, he'd send me and the other women to another bishop—Gethin Hughes of San Diego was mentioned—to be ordained. Bishop Schofield would then allow us to be licensed to minister in the Diocese of San Joaquin.

After my first interview with Bishop Schofield, I was invited, along with my husband, to attend a discernment weekend in May. This took place at the Episcopal Conference Center in Oakhurst (ECCO) and consisted of a series of intense interviews by members of the Commission on Ministry and the Standing Committee. The weekend went well, and I received a letter from Canon Thompson in June 2001, admitting me to the ordination process. I had my physical and psychological examinations that summer, and began to gather the other material needed.

As a postulant, I enjoyed the community of others who were in the process, and formed some wonderful friendships, especially with the other women who attended classes at the seminary in Fresno. Michele Racusin, a year ahead of me, offered good advice as I continued through the process. Suzy Ward, already a deacon, was also there, and had petitioned the bishop to be allowed to enter the priest track. Most of the other women who attended the Anglican Studies classes were working toward diaconal ordination, and a few were still in discernment. Some had no intention of seeking Holy Orders, but were working on improving their knowledge of the church and deepening their spiritual lives.

My best friend in seminary, however, was not a woman. George Cano was a fellow parishioner at St. Dunstan's, preparing for ordination as a deacon. He and his wife, Paige, became close friends as we dealt with the drama and conflict that seemed to be in the DNA of our parish. Father Morello delegated many tasks to us, and we were farther along than many of our classmates as a result. During the Anglican Studies phase of school, George was my travel buddy and we spent most of our drive to and from Fresno discussing theology and church politics, and solving the problems of the universe. And sometimes we just gossiped.

For me, the biggest betrayal committed by Bishop Schofield was when he did an about-face on women's ordination immediately after General Convention in 2003. At that historic event, Gene Robinson, an openly partnered gay man, was affirmed in his election as bishop of the Diocese of New Hampshire. All the deputies from San Joaquin, both clergy and lay, were instructed to vote "no" on the consent. However, I know that at least one clergy deputy voted "yes" and it cost him dearly. After the convention, he was removed from all diocesan committees, and even worse, for those who were Anglican Studies students, he was removed as a professor.

The bishop's response—to someone who had clearly voted the way the Holy Spirit had informed him—was typical: "Don't get mad, get even" was the way things worked in the diocese, and you never knew, from one moment to the next, whom you could trust. I was once talking about ordination to an elderly priest who had supplied at St. Dunstan's who seemed pleased that I was going to seminary, but before responding, slowly looked over his shoulders, one at a time, then all around the area in which we were conversing. Then he said, in a whisper, *"I'm really in favor of women's ordination, you know."* That told me a lot about the climate in which we lived—that a member of San Joaquin's clergy was afraid that someone might overhear him admit such a shocking thing.

When I traveled outside the Diocese of San Joaquin, however, it was a much different story. I took a trip to western New York with our son, Chris, not long after beginning the process. We visited an Episcopal Church on a Sunday, and I introduced myself to the deacon who had served at the altar that day. She took my hand in both of her own, and said, "Oh! I'm so sorry about what's going on in your diocese. We are all praying for you."

During the spring semester of 2004, I was told that I should soon be hearing from the diocesan office to schedule a meeting with the Standing Committee and the Commission on Ministry. I submitted answers to the middler evaluation I was given, and waited for a call from the vocations officer. By this time, Canon Thompson had left the diocese, moving to Oregon, and was replaced by the Reverend Van McAllister, who had been a seminary classmate of mine but had been on the fast track to ordination. After hearing nothing throughout the summer, I finally wrote to

Father McAllister and he eventually scheduled a meeting for early December 2004 for the purpose of advancing me to candidacy, the final step before ordination to the diaconate. By that time, it was clear to all the women in the process that there was no way that John-David Schofield would ever consent to allowing women to work as priests in his diocese, let alone ordain us to the priesthood. Michele Racusin had been ordained to the transitional diaconate, but the bishop was suggesting that she transfer to another conservative bishop's diocese where they actually had women priests. Other women who had previously been on the "priest track" were starting to reassess their discernment, deciding that they were, after all, called to the diaconate. One woman, who had won a tough battle to be accepted as a postulant, was convinced that John-David would make an exception in her case, since her vocation was to do missionary work in Africa. Another woman in a similar position had been ordained to the priesthood by an African bishop in an out-of-the-way setting in the strip of territory that was along the border between the Diocese of San Joaquin and the Diocese of Los Angeles. She was ordained to serve as a priest in Africa. She is currently assisting in a Methodist Church in the deep South. She is canonically resident in the Anglican Coalition of America.

By the time I'd completed my second year of my Master of Divinity program, I was finally able to face the fact that there was little likelihood of moving forward toward ordination. The events of the 2003 General Convention, followed by the vitriolic blogs by conservative followers of John-David and his ilk, plus the measured and amazingly patient and grace-filled responses by Bishop Gene Robinson, convinced me that it was time to look outside San Joaquin to the wider church. I recall being given a copy of *Ruach*, the publication of the Episcopal Women's Caucus.

Reading about the successful struggle for women's ordination in other parts of The Episcopal Church was uplifting to me, and I naively thought that those within the women's caucus would offer aid or support to the women of San Joaquin. I wrote a letter to the editor, telling her just a small fraction of what we were up against, expecting to get some type of action or at least some degree of sympathy, but I received no response. In retrospect, I think that what had been going on in San Joaquin for more than two decades was so incredible that the wider church just didn't believe it. After the schism, when many clergy and officers of The Episcopal Church came to visit, they told us as much. They thought that much of what they had been hearing over the years was an exaggeration—it couldn't possibly be as bad as all that.

One of the saddest results of the schism was the loss of so many fine women who had been ordained to the diaconate and compelled to remain with John-David Schofield after the split. Bishop Schofield told the deacons that they served at the discretion of the bishop and therefore they go where the bishop goes. Some of those women had been called to the priesthood, affirmed by COM, and working on their M.Divs., but gave up their vocation when they chose to become part of the Anglican Diocese of San Joaquin. Only two active deacons from the diocese remained in The Episcopal Church: George Cano of Christ the King, Riverbank, and Suzy Ward, who became the first woman ordained to the priesthood in the diocese.

In August, I met with a priest who I was hoping would serve as my spiritual director. The Reverend Richard Matters was the rector of St. John the Baptist in Lodi, and I told him my story and expressed frustration with being "stuck." With seminary graduation less than a year away, I wouldn't even get my middler evaluation and candidacy meeting until almost Christmas. Yet I heard of male colleagues in seminary who had been advanced to candidacy and had ordination dates set before they even completed their degree. Father Rick asked me, "Which diocese would you like to go to if you can't be ordained here: Northern California or California?" My preference was Northern California, for no other reason than I preferred the drive to Sacramento over the drive to San Francisco. Father Matters called the canon to the ordinary in Northern California first, and was told that they would prefer it if I could first be ordained to the diaconate before I tried to transfer. That meant waiting until the following year, at least. The bishop of California, William Swing, was traveling, but his canon promised to leave him a message about my situation. The following week, I received a phone call that Bishop Swing would like to meet me in his office and I drove to Grace Cathedral in San Francisco.

When I arrived, I was greeted by the receptionist. I told her my name and that I was there to meet with Bishop Swing. She responded, "Oh, you're the woman from the Diocese of San Quentin!" I laughed, and said, "No, Diocese of San Joaquin, but you're not far off." After hearing my story, Bishop Swing said, "Well, we'll just have to rescue you. You can transfer here and we'll get you through the rest of the process." One of the questions he asked me was about financial aid for seminary: "How much have you received from the Diocese of San Joaquin in scholarship or grant money?" I actually laughed at the question; no money had ever been offered or received, either for me or, as far as I knew, for any of the women in the process. I had heard rumors at school that some of the male students had a grant each semester to help with tuition and books, but I had never had the courage to ask any of them about it. They were also invited to seminars and retreats to help them learn about such ministries as church planting, but the women students were never asked to come. Bishop Swing looked startled, then angry at my response. He told me that there had been money set aside from the Diocese of California that was given to San Joaquin in order to help support seminarians. He sent me to the office of the archdeacon of the diocese, the Venerable Dorothy Jones, and told me that she had a list of scholarship recipients and that my name was on it. Sure enough, my name, along with other women from San Joaquin, was indeed on the list. The amount I had supposedly received wasn't much, but the fact that the Diocese of San Joaquin reported that they distributed money equally to male and female seminarians was a blatant lie.

Over the years, I'd heard a lot about "financial irregularities" within the Diocese of San Joaquin, but the fact that the leadership was also reporting false information to another diocese and bishop was over the top. It was another reason for me to accept Bishop Swing's invitation to come to his diocese. I began to explore options of where I would like to serve if I decided to make the move. The bishop had suggested that I continue to work toward being ordained to the diaconate in San Joaquin before transferring, but that if I were refused candidacy I would then transfer immediately to California, and that's exactly what happened in December 2004. The meeting for my candidacy was a farce. Although for the most part the meeting was cordial, one clergy member greeted me with a scowl and arms crossed, looking resentful and angry that I'd been allowed to get that far. In contrast, the president of Commission on Ministry was Ron Perry, the priest who'd been assigned as my mentor; he was conservative but not against women's ordination. He was very kind to me during the interview, and I felt at times that he was trying to direct the questioning in order to help me make a good impression. But to no avail. Soon it became clear to me that the primary questions they wanted me to answer centered on lesbian, gay, bisexual, and transgender people in the church, and on the possibility of schism from The Episcopal Church. I was asked by one member, since Bishop Schofield would not ordain me, where was I going to go? My response was that I would go where God called me. "Well, will just *any* diocese do?" I think it was about then that I thought, " They won't make me a candidate anyway, so I might as well let them know how I feel." And I did. A week later, I received the letter denying me candidacy and I transferred to the Diocese of California.

Bishop Swing suggested I "shop around" the Diocese of California in order to find a comfortable church to attend and do my field education while awaiting ordination. I visited St. Bartholomew's in Livermore, and stayed there for the duration, until I was accepted back into San Joaquin when Bishop Jerry arrived. St. Bart's was the perfect place for me. The Reverend Carol Cook was the rector and the Reverend Lyn Morlan was in the final stages prior to ordination to the priesthood when I arrived, so I had two wonderful women to mentor me there and a wonderful St. Bart's congregation. For about the first six months I sat there like a lump, not doing much of anything. In retrospect, I think I was suffering from post-traumatic stress after dealing with the strange goings-on at St. Dunstan's, and the trauma of not being able to finish the process in the diocese in which I felt the call to ministry. But I eventually recovered, and Carol put me on the preaching rotation. I also sang a lot—music is therapeutic for me, especially with the wonderful choir at St. Bart's. The biggest problem was living more than fifty miles from the church, so Sunday was about the only time I could be there, except during Holy Week and Christmas. Carol Cook has since retired, and the Reverend Lyn Morlan is now rector of St. Anne's in Stockton.

My ordinations were a marvel—when I first went to

San Francisco to see Bishop Swing, I walked around Grace Cathedral and thought I'd died and gone to heaven, and that's where I was ordained. Since it was Bishop Swing's last ordination, everyone in the process wanted to be ordained at the same time, so there were about twenty of us ordained to the diaconate on June 3, 2006. Then, we were all priested by Bishop Marc Andrus, newly elected, on December 2, 2006.

At a Remain Episcopal event that took place at Christ the King, Riverbank, in 2007, we had a small-group breakout session in order to discuss the presentation Fathers Paul Colbert and Glenn Kanestrom made. I led the discussion, and when it was time for a break, one of the gentlemen in our group wanted to talk to me. He explained he was a breakaway Anglican but was curious to know if what he was told about The Episcopal Church was true. He'd heard that church doesn't believe in the divinity of Jesus Christ, that we rarely read the Bible, that we don't believe what the Bible says—and more. This came as quite a shock to me that clergy and lay leaders who practiced Christianity would spread such false information and demonize us. I did my best to reassure the man that most Episcopalians are pretty orthodox in our theology and worship. We do read the Bible often and study it seriously. He listened politely and thanked me. The very next presentation was done by Father Basil Matthews, who spoke about the importance of deepening our relationship to Christ by using spiritual practices that have been used by Christians for hundreds of years. As I listened to Basil speak, I felt that the Holy Spirit was present and I hoped the man who had questioned me stayed to listen. No one could have demonstrated the true Anglican/Episcopal ethos better than Basil did that day. It turned out that the man had been listening and he and his family are very involved in an Episcopal Church in the Episcopal Diocese of San Joaquin. This story reveals God's abundant grace in resurrecting our diocese. Thanks be to God.

Tracy, California
June 2011

Coming Home

Carolyn Louise Woodall

Carolyn Louise Woodall, bishop's warden at St. Mary in the Mountains, Sonora, and chair of the diocesan Commission on Equality, is a deacon. She had been a postulant for the diaconate and attended the School for Deacons in 1993, also participating in the education program for deacons in formation that existed then. Carolyn is a deputy to General Convention and has served on Diocesan Council. She is an attorney who works as a deputy public defender in Tuolumne County. She has two children, Shawna and Lauren.

On March 29, 2008, I came home.

I'd been away from The Episcopal Church for six years, and feared I'd never be able to go back so long as I lived in the Diocese of San Joaquin. When former Bishop John-David Schofield attempted to take most of the diocese out of The Episcopal Church, it was a tragic day for many who were not willing to leave their church—for them it was an event filled with pain, heartbreak, and suffering. For me, it was a sign of hope, because the reason I fled The

Episcopal Church in 2002 was I no longer felt part of it.

What could cause a forty-eight-year-old, almost-cradle Episcopalian to leave her church? Bigotry, intolerance, condescension, and arrogance, to name a few reasons, from the diocesan leadership and most of the clergy. At my end it was an intense feeling of rejection. I was starting to realize at the time that I might be transsexual. I had been very good at self-denial for many years, but it was growing more difficult. And in the Diocese of San Joaquin, as it existed in 2002, there was no place for me.

It was in 2002, while attending St. Dunstan's in Modesto, that I had a serious falling-out with the rector. It was serious enough that I felt I had to leave that congregation, but I faced a huge quandary. I didn't know of any nearby Episcopal Church where I could feel welcome, or even comfortable, even if I just tried to stay under the radar. Not that staying under the radar would have been difficult just then. I still wasn't fully admitting to myself that I was transsexual, that I was transgender. Somewhere inside of me I knew, but I figured it was just occasional cross-dressing and not a big deal. I also didn't plan to tell anyone about any of it.

But in San Joaquin in those days, contempt for those who were gay or lesbian was fairly openly expressed—from the bishop on down to most of the priests. If my gay friends had issues, what was I going to face if anyone found out about me?

My friend William had left the church some months before this. I told him about my falling out with the rector and he invited me to attend Emanuel Lutheran with him. I thought that was a good idea, since I saw no place for me in the Diocese of San Joaquin and that's where I lived. I had visited Emanuel once before when William invited me to hear a special piece the choir was singing. The liturgy was close enough that I could be comfortable and the people seemed nice enough.

The pastor was Paul Bodin, a caring and loving man who intimidated me with the depth of his intellect. The associate pastor, Barbara Caine, is one of those people with infectious optimism and enthusiasm. She's also the reason I'm alive to write this story. That thought makes her uncomfortable to this day, but it is the fact of the matter.

After my first Sunday at Emanuel I was pressed into service in the choir. I threw myself into it with glee. We had a good choir and a fantastic organist. I began serving as an assisting minister—a cross between eucharistic minister and deacon as far as liturgical duties went. Life was good.

Then one day in 2002, when my wife called to tell me she wanted a separation, my world fell apart. The reason, she said, was financial, though it later turned out that she thought I was gay. I was actually hoping she was right. If you're gay, you see, you can stay in the closet fairly easily at work. We left it there for a while and shared a house for financial reasons, but after my next raise she insisted I find my own place.

In February 2003 I moved to a one-bedroom cottage in the middle of the woods in Tuolumne County. The day I moved in I was devastated. I still loved my wife and keenly felt the loss when the front door of what was once my home closed behind me.

But I did my best to settle in. Not too long after the move I had a talk with Pastor Barbara because I was feeling depressed. I also told her there was a possibility I was gay. She said a lot of people thought so because I was such good friends with William, but she made it clear that it wasn't a problem as far as the church was concerned. Since part of what I was talking to her about was being depressed over the separation, she asked me if I was having any thoughts of suicide (with the mandatory notifications attached to the question). I told her that the day I was told my wife wanted to separate I considered it in passing, but not seriously, and that was months in the past. Nevertheless, she asked me to promise that if I ever had such feelings I would call her, no matter what day or time. I told her I would. She said that wasn't enough; she wanted my promise. I gave my promise.

I started reading books about being gay and Christian, and was pretty much reconciled to that as a possibility, as a hope. I was, even then, trying to deny being transsexual. I was also trying to get some sense of normalcy in my new life. But that didn't work out well.

One Sunday night in April 2003, I was sitting at my desk writing in my journal, a practice I'd started after I moved. At my bedroom desk, I'd light a few candles, turn off the lights, and write about my day, thoughts, and feelings until I was ready to turn in. I was writing about that being the day that I quit fooling myself. I was transsexual and I needed to deal with it. I guess my inhibitions were finally down. My parents had died by then, and I was living on my own. That day the realization of who I truly was came fully out, along with the realization that I needed to do something about it. I saw two options: I could learn to live with it, start living as a woman, and move on with life, or I could kill myself.

I decided on suicide that night. I sat there convinced of a couple of things. One was that I was an abomination before God. I had long before given up anything remotely resembling a literalist view of the Bible, I knew that the law was fulfilled in Christ, and I was a gentile besides, so being an abomination didn't apply to me because I wasn't Jewish. So why did I feel this way? Partly it was because God made me male at birth and I would be unfaithful to God by changing that. Plus, even though I'd learned a lot about people, and had transsexual friends, it was about me this time, not someone else. No intellectual rationalization could overcome the feelings that had been instilled in me since I was little and first expressed an interest in things feminine. This was wrong. So was suicide, but that night I prayed that God would consider suicide the lesser sin and forgive me for what I was about to do.

The other reason was my children. If I killed myself rather than transition at least they could tell their friends that their dad was dead rather than that their dad was a woman—it seemed like that would be easier on them. So my decision was made. I had a gun in the dresser right behind me and it would be quick and easy.

I stood up, trembling and scared but determined, but I realized I'd forgotten something important. I'd promised Pastor Barbara that I'd call her if I ever had the urge to kill myself. My exact thought was, "She will kill me if I don't call and say goodbye." I was in such bad shape that I didn't even groan over that thought—either the absurdity of it or the fact that I needed to call to say goodbye rather than ask for help. But I couldn't call her. She was on vacation and I couldn't reach her. I'd have to wait until she got back. I went to bed.

The next morning I woke to the horror of what I'd almost done the night before, and was frightened at the thought that I'd only decided to postpone it because I couldn't keep my promise to Pastor Barbara. I quickly realized that I'd been looking for a reason not to go through with it and was very glad I'd found one.

I started seeing a therapist and, in many ways, began my life over again. I told the therapist that I thought I was gay and was depressed. We had a long talk about that. She suggested that I make contact with the LGBT community in Sonora, the city where I work. That community is larger than you might suppose, but mostly underground. I went to a meeting of a group called "Out in the Mother Lode." I sat in my car for quite a while first, but I finally went in. I was early so the only person there was Jerry Cadotte, who ran the meeting. Others drifted in and I actually enjoyed myself.

When I returned to my therapist I finally told her that I was pretty sure I was transsexual rather than gay. It was a hard thing to say and I think I skirted the issue for about forty minutes. Even though I had faced it squarely that awful night, I'd resolved, at the time, not to live with it. Now I had to face being transsexual with the resolve to live with it. That meant, if I was right about who I thought I was, leaving behind the life I had built and embarking on a journey into unknown and dangerous territory. I was under no delusions about the difficulty of transitioning from an established life as a man to one as a woman. I also knew that having to make that transition was going to be the likely consequence of starting that journey. Not everyone has to go so far, but I'd truly taken a good, hard, and honest look at myself and knew that I would.

That knowledge was reinforced in my therapy sessions. We explored my past and looked for times in my childhood consistent with being a girl forced to live as a boy. There were a lot of them, most of which I'd shoved away in a dark corner of my brain. They were usually accompanied by guilt, expressions of disappointment by my parents, or the knowledge that if they ever found out I'd be letting them down. There was a lot of digging to do, a lot of reconciliation, and a lot of self-esteem building.

Neither did we neglect the spiritual side of the issue. My therapist encouraged me to tell Pastor Barbara and, finally, in the summer of 2003, I did. I was frightened. I knew, intellectually, that she'd accept this, but I'd spent so many years inwardly cowering in fear of being transsexual that on an emotional level I had doubts about her being able to accept it.

We met for dinner and somewhere in the middle of the meal I dropped the bomb. I told her that I was transsexual. My fears turned out to be unfounded. She had dealt with this before. She wasn't shocked, didn't feel revulsion, and was optimistic about my ability to deal with it. We talked about my fears about God. We talked about the seeming blasphemy of rejecting the body God had given me. She reminded me that I was God's creation—all of me. If my soul was female, it was because God created it so. The male body, well that was more of a challenge, but she said it could be an opportunity for spiritual growth. It was, but there's a funny thing about spiritual growth—sometimes it comes with growing pains.

I continued my therapy and my discussions with Pastor Barbara. My therapist was satisfied that I was genuinely transsexual and gave me a letter recommending hormone therapy, which involves taking estrogen along with another drug to suppress testosterone production. This was a big step because the hormone therapy causes some physical changes. For about three months the physical effects are reversible by simply stopping. After that, permanent changes start to take place. I had also started electrolysis to start to get rid of my beard.

With all this going on, I decided I needed to tell Pastor Paul, so I met with him in the fall of 2003. He had some knowledge of transgender issues and was very supportive. We talked about my eventual external transition to being Carolyn in church, though at the time I'd planned to wait almost an additional year for that step. I changed my mind as the hormones started to kick in and I was actually enjoying everything that was happening. I decided that there was no need to wait too long. I was on the path I was meant to follow, and there was no need for delay. Besides, according to the medical standards, before I could get the surgery done I had to live as a woman for a full year.

I talked with Pastor Paul and with Pastor Barbara about the details as I'd decided to go gradually, starting with church. I suggested a period of education before I showed up as Carolyn, with an announcement in advance of what would happen. The Executive Committee felt that wouldn't be the best approach—instead, they suggested a few people be told and let the rumor mill take it from there. I told them they were wrong and it turned out, they were. On January 18, 2004, I showed up at the 8:15 a.m. service, guitar in hand, as Carolyn and took people by surprise. The choir sang at the 11:00 a.m. service. I had a solo, and when people turned around to look up into the choir loft—well, some of the reactions were priceless. So much for the rumor mill.

As a result of the furor, the next week Pastor Paul had to do what I'd suggested he should have done in the first place—explain the situation to everyone. I'd been very much afraid the approach chosen would be a bad one, with some adverse reactions. I'd thoroughly researched the issues involved in coming out as transsexual and dealing with the public transition. If you drop the bomb, you get caught in the explosion. The furor died down and most people worked very hard to understand what was happening. Unfortunately, I think it left those who were inclined to have difficulty accepting me with an enhanced feeling of negativity.

Shortly after my public transition at church (work would be a couple of months away), there were a series of meetings at people's homes. The purpose was to discuss what was going on in the church—the good, the not so good, and what people wanted to see happen. Not surprisingly I was a hot topic. There was to be a congregational meeting to discuss the group discussions, and Pastor Barbara told me there was a whole section about me and that several negative comments had been made. She e-mailed them to me with the assurance that she would understand if I didn't come to church the next day. The comments left me devastated and I did stay home. She told me later that many of the critics were quite chagrined as she had written their statements verbatim and they were hearing the comments they made being read back to them. She pointed out to the group that I was not at the meeting. In response to a suggestion that perhaps I stayed home so people could talk freely, she replied that was a possibility, but not a safe one upon which to bet. She was telling them, if they were willing to read between the lines, that I was absent because I was hurt.

Only a small group of people had said hurtful things, but it precipitated a crisis for me. I realized that I was hurting my church and was clearly not welcomed by everyone. The next time I went to Emanuel was for the Lenten Tuesday soup supper. I made the hour-long drive to Modesto from Sonora, so I usually arrived just in time to miss supper and catch the program and the Taizé service. As I approached the door to the parish hall that night it felt like there was a tangible barrier over it. I went in anyway and sat in the back of the room, but I couldn't stay. I went into the sanctuary and sat in a pew until everything was over and the choir came in to practice. I left and went to talk to Pastor Barbara. After a time she took me up to the choir loft and told everyone I was having some problems and needed to be welcomed—and they all did.

It got me back into the church, but the process left a wound that God had to heal. It doesn't take many people to turn a loving and accepting congregation into a hostile one. Although most people will be oblivious to it, hostility toward someone is readily discernible if you are that someone. It does not take much of being the target of hostility for it to overcome that which is positive and supportive. The congregational meeting had exposed what might otherwise have festered and grown over time. Having the issues of my transition out in the open helped me tremendously over the next several weeks. My self-confidence had been sorely wounded. The most serious part of it was that my self-confidence included my belief that I was acceptable to God as I was—as Carolyn. When a church—even a part of it—rejects you for who you are, it can affect your relationship not only with the church but with God. I came through this, with time, prayer, therapy, and many talks with Pastor Barbara. I came through stronger, thanks be to God.

My next step was to complete the transition at work. Work presented an entirely different set of challenges. I was, and still am, a deputy public defender in a rural mountain county. My name was well known due to the size of the county and my being mentioned in the paper whenever I had a high-profile case. So my transition there was public. Not only was it in the local paper, but it eventually became a two-page article, with color pictures, in the Modesto Bee's Sunday edition in June 2004. That's how most of the people I'd known from my years in Modesto found out about my transition.

After the excitement of my transition to living full time as Carolyn died down, life continued on fairly normally. I was busy at work and at church. I was continuing in my therapy and preparing for the next step—surgery. In the meantime, things changed significantly at church. Emanuel was experiencing some financial difficulties and one way to save money was to cut back to one pastor. Rather than just let Pastor Barbara go, they both decided to make themselves available for a call and the first one called elsewhere would go. That ended up being Pastor Barbara. Her last day at Emanuel was a tough one for me. She'd been my pastor, my friend, my rock, and she was leaving. She wasn't going far, just to Newark, California, but that was far enough. I took some solace in the fact that I could still visit her.

I stayed busy at Emanuel, continuing in the choir and as an assisting minister. I also took a position on the council, which is similar to the vestry in The Episcopal Church. During this time, I was also preparing for my surgery—I'd be eligible for surgery as of March 30, 2005. All I needed was my second letter of recommendation and money.

Early on the morning of July 29, 2005, my friend Merri, who was going to look after me after the surgery, and I went to the Menlo Park Surgical Hospital. We met Pastor Barbara there and my friends Evelyn and Fred came by as well. When everything was ready, we prayed and I walked to the O.R. I woke up in the recovery room several hours later with the surgery completed and Merri and Pastor Barbara waiting for me. The next couple of weeks were interesting and, at times, remarkably painful, but healing happened and I returned to work after about five weeks.

A few months later, Pastor Paul accepted a new position at a church in Spokane. I know that churches survive clergy changes, and I've been through it a few times with minimal trauma. But this was an unusual circumstance. Pastor Paul and Pastor Barbara had helped me cope with a change in life that most people can't even begin to understand or imagine. I'd not only lived through it but came through much stronger than before—especially regarding my faith in God. Now they'd both be gone.

Living as I did in Sonora, and growing tired of the commute, I decided I might as well start going to Mt. Calvary Lutheran Church in Sugar Pine, about fifteen miles up the hill. I was well received there, but it just wasn't a good fit—I always felt like a visitor. So I decided to look for a new church, especially since I'd moved from Sonora to Copperopolis, an hour's drive from Sugar Pine.

Over the course of a year I'd tried several churches, looking, without much success, for a place that was a fit. I was missing The Episcopal Church, and had kept an eye on what was happening in the diocese. When I read about the special convention in March 2008, I knew I had to go. I was more than ready to come home and I needed to know if it would be safe.

I went with two purposes. One was to assess the state of the diocese following the schism. The other was to see if I could safely come back and be accepted as I am. That would entail running into people who knew me back when I was male. It would require that I try to get an idea of what the general attitudes were going to be about LGBT people. The fact that I am back indicates how things went, but some specifics are in order.

The Most Reverend Katharine Jefferts Schori, our presiding bishop, attended the convention and spoke at length. As I listened to her message—that we all have differences but we have a commonality in Christ that overshadows all of our differences—I knew it was safe, at last, to come home. God lived in the reconstituted Diocese of San Joaquin. The whole day was so moving that when it was finally at an end I rushed out the door, shook Bishop Katharine's hand, thanked her for being there, and rushed off before I started crying.

Her message was given life by other happenings at the convention. I was greeted warmly by all who'd stayed with The Episcopal Church. I saw that Integrity had a booth. I was once told that there were attempts to start an Integrity chapter in the diocese and that former Bishop Schofield crashed the meeting and proclaimed there was no Integrity in the Diocese of San Joaquin. The tale may be true or not, but the double entendre is a telling comment on the troubled diocese. But that day in 2008, the booth was a positive sign to me.

That day I was also invited to St. Mary in the Mountains in Sonora. I'd heard of St. Mary's, but I was afraid to go. Having to fight for myself and my right to exist as a woman, I'd seen people direct their fear and hatred at me. I can deal with their rejection, but it carries a particularly painful sting when it comes from a church. So I'd learned to approach new churches with trepidation if I approached them at all. But my experience at that special convention, and the invitation to attend St. Mary's, were enough to convince me that the time had come to take the risk.

The next morning when I walked in the door of St. Mary's for the first time, I was surprised to see Stan Coppel, the parish's deacon. I knew him from his days as a bailiff in the courts. He saw me and said, "Am I ever glad to see you here." I decided that I was glad to see me there, too. The rest of the congregation had the same attitude and I had found a home.

After a few weeks I started getting a bit more comfortable—a typical process of getting to know the people and the dynamics of the place. I was comfortable enough to ask if I could make a parish website. After a while I offered to play guitar when our pianist was gone, and I began to sing in the choir. I visited a Bishop's Committee meeting to propose we join in sponsoring the Resolution on Equality being proposed for the 2008 Diocesan Convention. The next month I found myself on the Bishop's Committee to fill a vacancy—the junior warden. I also started serving as a eucharistic minister.

As my life at St. Mary's progressed, I started to feel something that had lain dormant since I'd left St. Dunstan's—a desire to pursue ordained ministry. I had been a postulant for the diaconate before, and dropped out of the process because of my growing concerns over my gender identity issues. I knew that former Bishop Schofield would never ordain me if he knew, and I couldn't move forward if I didn't tell him, so I left the process. The call to ordained ministry was something I'd never felt during my time with the ELCA, where I was content to be part of the choir and be an assisting minister.

I talked to Deacon Stan about it, and to Father Martin Risard, our vicar. He told me he wasn't surprised—he saw a vocation in me. I'd had others ask when I was going to start seminary. Sometimes I *can* take a hint, and the support and encouragement I received were necessary to me.

While I was dealing with all of this at St. Mary's, our first convention as a reconstituted diocese happened, where a resolution was introduced establishing a Commission on Equality to examine the marginalization that had been a part of the diocese under former Bishop Schofield, explore ways to bring the marginalized into full participation as members and leaders in the diocese, and report findings to the next convention. I addressed the convention, telling them I was part of the LGBT community and that I'd had to leave The Episcopal Church because of the policies of the previous diocesan leadership. I emphasized that the commission was necessary—we needed to ensure that the things that had happened under Bishop Schofield's tenure would never happen again.

The Commission on Equality was formed and in March 2009 we had our first meeting, and I served as chair. We submitted a modest report to the next convention—fifty pages or so chronicling stories of rejection, belittling, fear, and anguish.We talked about the problems experienced by those of different races and cultures, by women, by the disabled, and by those who were lesbian, gay, bisexual, and transgender. We learned that people wanted education about the issues faced by those who had been marginalized, and that Bishop Lamb was considered to be a gift from God for pulling our remnants back into a diocese. We spent the next year traveling the diocese, sharing our findings. We could never go back to what was before. We had moved from the twelfth century into the twenty-first in a very short time. It was a move that we embraced, and we continue to move forward.

I'm now in the process for ordination to the diaconate. Throughout my journey, I had to challenge one of the more fundamental aspects of societal differentiation—the difference between male and female—and survive. God helped me survive, and so did Emanuel Lutheran. Had I stayed in The Episcopal Church in the years leading up to the schism, I probably would have taken my life that night in 2003. But there were people who loved and cherished me for who I was. I want others to know this, and to experience the care and concern I did when I most needed it. I want others to experience the welcoming community I found when I returned to The Episcopal Church.

Although we are still working at it, I am happy to be able to say that the Diocese of San Joaquin is now one of those welcoming places. On March 29, 2008, I came home and I am here to stay.

Sonora, California
June 2011

Endnote: On March 10, 2012, Carolyn Louise Woodall was ordained to the diaconate by Bishop Chester Talton.

Marginalized
but Faithful

John Ledbetter

John Ledbetter was senior warden for three years at St. John the Baptist Episcopal Church in Lodi, California. During this period of turmoil in the Diocese of San Joaquin, St. John's was also searching for a full-time rector. The vestry worked closely with Remain Episcopal and counsel Michael Glass, attempting to bring attention to the situation in the diocese. John and St. John's Episcopal Church were intimately involved in hosting the special convention to elect Jerry Lamb as provisional bishop. John served on the initial Standing Committee of the continuing Diocese of San Joaquin for three years.

The beginning of the journey of St. John the Baptist Episcopal Church of Lodi, California, to Remain Episcopal began many years before the official vote at the December 2007 Diocese of San Joaquin convention. It began in the late 1980s, not long into Bishop John-David Schofield's reign of terror as bishop of San Joaquin.

St. John's rector, the Reverend Ray Knapp, had retired after seventeen years of service, and after a period of time with supply priests, the bishop's office sent an interim priest to our parish as we began the search process. He did a reasonable job leading St. John's, but it became evident that he wouldn't be a good long-term fit.

During a visit, Bishop Schofield met with the vestry and the congregation at an open forum. We asked about the search process and the role of the bishop's office and about how long the interim priest would be with us. Untruthful with us for the first time, Bishop Schofield responded, "He will not be considered in your search process as the rector of St. John's."

So our search continued without success in finding someone we could call as our full-time rector. St. John's was willing to continue the process, but before we knew it, Bishop Schofield proclaimed that the interim would now be our rector.

At the time, our parish wasn't experienced in the process of resisting the will of the bishop. After all, our past encounters with the bishop's office had been lovingly above board under the leadership of Bishop Victor Rivera. There was no reason to believe that Bishop Schofield didn't have St. John's best interests at heart, so our congregation went along with the bishop and accepted the appointed rector.

But this was the beginning of a long, slow, thoughtful, intentional process of Bishop Schofield replacing priests in parishes throughout the Diocese of San Joaquin. Over the following ten years or so, it became evident who was in Bishop Schofield's camp and who was not—and there seemed to be preferential treatment given to priests and parishes who were in the John-David Schofield camp.

The handpicked interim forced on our congregation lasted for only a short time. We began to develop some courage and started the search process again. Over a period of about eighteen months, we called a new rector, the Reverend

Richard (Rick) Matters.

The process of bringing into the diocese those loyal to Bishop Schofield filtered into other leadership positions. By the December 2007 convention, the bishop had loaded the deck of cards in his favor by handpicking the Diocesan Council and the Standing Committee. Though he didn't support ordination of women, he did accept ordained women in residence to the diocese so they could support his ideals. By the end of his tenure, most of the ordained clergy who disagreed with the bishop had retired or left the Diocese of San Joaquin for other callings.

Father Rick was with St. John's for about fourteen years, leaving us for a new calling in June 2006. During his tenure, St. John's relationship with the bishop's office and the hand-chosen leadership of the diocese became more distant. In more ways than one, we were feeling the effects of being the most northern parish in the Diocese of San Joaquin.

Under the leadership of Father Rick, St. John's experienced a period of growth and transition, which led to our decision to build a new church building on the edge of Lodi on Lower Sacramento Road. During the four years of planning, a capital campaign, and the construction of our new building, there wasn't one word of encouragement from the bishop's office. Since ours was the only parish to build a new worship facility under John-David Schofield's term as bishop, it was natural to expect some support. But as senior warden, I saw first-hand how our rector and congregation were ignored and marginalized by the bishop's office and diocesan leadership. We didn't fall into line with the Bishop Schofield school of thought, and the process of being ignored worsened.

During Father Rick's years at St. John's, he taught a valuable lesson by his actions and words. As disagreements in the larger church were becoming more apparent and Bishop Schofield more controversial, one of Father Rick's messages to our congregation was that we all don't have to agree with one another on every issue, but we all do need to worship together in a respectful and loving way. This message carried St. John's through some dark days and it's the reason we were one of only a handful of parishes that made it through the split as a complete parish.

When Father Rick was called to a new congregation in the spring of 2006, I was again senior warden. Our vestry was strong and united, but we were quickly put to the test. Father Rick departed on a Sunday and the next evening was our normally scheduled vestry meeting. But that morning the canon to the ordinary called, asking to get together to "discuss your open rector position" and ways for the diocese to "help you in your search process." The canon and the diocesan chief financial officer said that "since the bishop knows you so well, we can short-circuit the search process and save you time and money." The bishop's solution was for us to just accept his hand-picked priest as our rector. We listened to the bishop's representatives, then explained that we were already in the process of preparing the church profile and that our congregation thought it would be healthy for us to complete it. The diocesan representatives responded that the parishioners of St. John's congregation would leave because of no diocesan support and that we would have to close the church doors (again the intimidation factor). They offered to "keep in touch," but we never heard from them again.

With this parting of the ways, St. John's knew where we stood with the bishop. Our vestry was assisting the financial support of the Remain Episcopal movement. We were in conversation with the Remain Episcopal counsel Michael Glass, who wisely advised us of the church canons.

These were challenging times for St. John's. We were without a rector and had no support from the bishop's office. But the Holy Spirit led Father Basil Matthews to us as a part-time interim priest. Father Basil was just what our congregation needed—a healing soul who preached God's love for all. His message, in combination with what Father Rick had taught us, sustained our congregation during our search for a rector, helped us deal with the split in our diocese, and led to the ultimate involvement of the presiding bishop's office.

Finally, Remain Episcopal and Michael Glass got the attention of the national leadership about the plight of the Diocese of San Joaquin and the direction Bishop Schofield was going. Bonnie Anderson, president of the House of Deputies, came to visit our diocese in the fall of 2007 to listen and deliver a message of support from Presiding Bishop Katharine. Bishop Schofield attended this meeting, but said nothing. He was there again to intimidate those loyal to Remain Episcopal.

Several hundred Episcopalians gathered at St. John's for this special day. Tears of sadness and joy were shed; we came to realize how emotionally and spiritually exhausted we were. Bonnie Anderson's visit gave us hope for the future of the Diocese of San Joaquin—and our hopes were fulfilled on March 29, 2008, when Bishop Jerry Lamb was elected and seated by Presiding Bishop Katharine as our provisional bishop.

That special day was the beginning of the healing process for St. John's and the continuing Diocese of San Joaquin. We were privileged to be the host congregation for the special convention and I was honored to be the cross bearer in this celebration procession leading Presiding Bishop Katharine, President Bonnie Anderson, and Bishop Jerry Lamb, the clergy, special guests, and a combined diocesan choir. Even today, I remember the emotion of the four hundred people who were there. History was made that day.

Before the split of the Diocese of San Joaquin, especially the last couple of years, it was very painful to attend Diocesan Conventions. Parishes and individuals who wanted to and ultimately chose to Remain Episcopal were disrespected, ignored, and marginalized. It was difficult to understand how a bishop and his followers could treat folks in such a hurtful way in a Christian setting.

After the special convention to elect and seat Bishop Jerry, I attended the regular Diocesan Conventions as a delegate representing St. John's. These conventions were a joy to attend—they were spiritual, loving, joyful, uplifting, and just plain fun. Lots of work was done, but there was also social time, storytelling, and sharing. We found that we'd all shared some dark times, but the light was beginning to shine through.

The predominant emotion after the first convention and the start of the diocese was relief and joy to be under the leadership of Bishop Jerry. It was necessary for the attendees to go through the process of telling their stories to finally begin the process of letting go. A year later, at our second convention, most people had let go of the past and eagerly looked forward to working toward our new future, joyful in once again being part of a larger community led by the Holy Spirit.

Reflecting back over the past ten years or so, the times that seemed the darkest and most hopeless were actually filled with the Holy Spirit. Remain Episcopal was alive and was truly being led by the Holy Spirit tirelessly shining light on the situation in the Diocese of San Joaquin. Our situation was difficult for those outside the diocese to understand.

The story of the continuing Diocese of San Joaquin truly is a story of resurrection. At times there were dark days as we felt abandoned and even close to death. But then there was light in the form of Remain Episcopal, Michael Glass, Bonnie Anderson, courageous laity, courageous clergy, and, in the end, Presiding Bishop Katharine. Her office brought us Bishop Jerry and Jane Lamb, sent to the Diocese of San Joaquin by God. Their loving and unselfish dedication during what were to be their retirement years has lifted the Diocese of San Joaquin from the valley of death.

It was a privilege and an honor for me to serve on the Standing Committee with Jerry Lamb as bishop. His spiritual leadership led the way for me and countless others to a new understanding and appreciation of the Holy Spirit, and I am deeply grateful to him.

Lodi, California
May 2011

Marching in the Light of God

Glenn Kanestrom

The Reverend Glenn Kanestrom is rector of Christ the King Episcopal Church in Riverbank. He is a member of the Standing Committee and a delegate to General Convention.

There is a wonderful bass solo in Handel's *Messiah* that puts to music the words of Isaiah: "Those who have walked in darkness have seen a great light." It is Handel's genius that the musical line of the melody fits the words so well: The melody is somewhat strange and irregular, and it gives you the feeling that you are stumbling around in the dark, not able to get a solid foothold, groping for the light. That image paints an accurate picture of my experience of being in the Diocese of San Joaquin.

I came to the diocese toward the end of 2002 and felt that, though I'd heard that the bishop was somewhat "isolationist," I wouldn't have much of a problem. The parish I'd come to, Christ the King, was conservative but the people were warm and my wife and I fell in love with the worship space and liked the Modesto area. As rumblings of schism began to be felt in 2005 or 2006, those of us who wanted no part of it quickly found one another for support. Father Rick Matters, Father Mark Hall, Father Joel Miller, and I met regularly to talk over what Remain Episcopal was doing, what the church leadership was doing to respond to our problems, and whether Bishop Schofield was really going to do this incredibly destructive thing. Was it a ploy, some kind of brinksmanship? Was he really that determined? Would he be physically strong enough to pull this off? These clergy meetings were at once scary—yes, it looked like he was doing it, and no, The Episcopal Church didn't seem to be doing much—and motivating, as my friends and I felt encouraged to step forward to resist this insanity. Stumble, grope.

It was also difficult for me to get a foothold in the parish. There were many who opposed the consecration of Gene Robinson and had trouble reconciling Christianity and homosexuality. There was a general distrust of the new presiding bishop, Katharine. Yet there were some free thinkers, and they were strong leaders. My plan was to communicate what I knew was going on in the diocese to the parish and to be open about these events. We had regular between-service gatherings to talk about the 2003 General Convention, we studied the Windsor Report, and we discussed all news from the bishop. All the while, I was weighing the attitude of the parish, gauging its mood and how the congregation would respond if the schism actually occurred. I wanted to be honest about how I felt, and yet I didn't want to lose the parish, nor my ability to serve the congregation pastorally. When was the time right to be prophetic?

As the 2007 convention approached, with the encouragement of our deacon, George Cano, and our senior warden, Norrel Stephen, I decided to lay my cards on the table and I told the parish that I would not vote to leave The Episcopal Church. I would remain true to my ordination vows: The Episcopal Church was my church. I said that I thought schism was an extreme action, that all other options for reconciliation had not been exhausted and that schism would damage the fabric of relationships in the diocese in ways that may never be mended. I said that there would be no parish vote as to whether we would remain in The Episcopal Church—we already were and would remain so. And so I cast my vote at convention, one of twelve against schism. And, amazingly, most of the congregation stayed.

There was a terrible period of waiting and not knowing what would happen after the schismatic Diocesan Convention and before the Executive Council geared up to help us begin again. The ground was unstable and the way filled with obstacles: Would Bishop Schofield swoop in and take Christ the King? Were the remaining Episcopalians just going to melt away? Could there be a diocese—and how? What was the way forward? Then, in mid-March 2008 John-David Schofield was deposed by the House of Bishops. Finally, with word of a special convention to seat a new provisional bishop, we found great hope. We set to work creating this convention, making sure it would be a time for the remaining Episcopalians to rally together and have some fun. There was much to do in a very short time, and when the special convention arrived I was physically and emotionally exhausted. At one point Bishop Jerry Lamb asked me in the middle of that service, "Are you all right?" Yes, I was tired but very, very happy. Here was light!

What was perhaps even more incredible was the news that the presiding bishop would come to Christ the King the next day to preach and celebrate at our Sunday Eucharist. Wow! As she was celebrating, I realized that Presiding Bishop Katharine was the first woman to either preach or celebrate at the altar of Christ the King. Again, a great light. Here at last was a solid foundation on which to stand.

We had a good turnout for her visit, considering

the short notice. There were some 150 souls that day and, though this was heartening, I also noticed that a number of parishioners were not there—and it was more than the "usual suspects." That was Sunday. On Monday I picked up a message on my phone from the senior warden with some disturbing news. The rector emeritus of Christ the King (and a follower of John-David) had been making calls. He had gone through the parish list and called people to tell them that he was starting a new "Anglican" parish in Modesto, and they were invited. I felt like the rug had been pulled out from under me.

Within the next few weeks, more and more parishioners were leaving Christ the King for the "other" church. When the dust settled we had lost thirty parishioners. I was heartbroken to realize that most of the children were gone as well. I tried to talk to each of these departing parishioners after I heard the news. They were friendly, said they liked Christ the King and would stay in touch, but they had made up their minds to leave. This was a dark time for me.

I'd had a "peaceable kingdom" idea about how the church should be, with different types and stripes all joining together around the common table and common cup. I'd had an idea that, as painful as it may be, it's better to have varied opinions and perspectives aired as we seek to do God's will. And I still feel this way, but there can be no place for bigotry or animosity at the table. And though variety is nice, unity is even nicer. Christ the King has become a far more unified church after these parishioners left.

So Christ the King Episcopal Church continues on. We are still rebuilding. We have welcomed some new families, and we seem to be on a much more solid footing. We march on together, marching in the light of God.

Riverbank, California
March 2011

All Are Welcome

John Shumaker

The Reverend John H. Shumaker has served within the Diocese of San Joaquin in San Andreas since 2001. Remaining faithful to The Episcopal Church in her traditions and ethos, Father John continued to minister throughout the schism within the diocese, even with the threats of removal by the former bishop. After the schism and reorganization of the diocese, he was elected to the Standing Committee at Diocesan Convention, and continues as Gold Country missioner within the Sierra Foothills.

On September 20, 2007, Bishop John-David Schofield invited me to meet him for lunch in Stockton, as he was on his way back from San Francisco. We had a delightful visit, and talked about the happenings within our parish and in the diocese. Everything seemed to be the usual friendly and jovial visit, until about ten minutes before the end of lunch. Abruptly, he stopped the small talk and said that we were having lunch together for a specific reason. As rector of St. Matthew's Church, I was being given one week to leave the parish, which he was changing to mission status at the next Diocesan Council. He also said that he was removing our deacon, a faithful parishioner who had received diaconal orders during my cure as rector, and transferring him until I was gone from the parish. This became a rallying point for our parish family.

This news was devastating to me and to our entire parish family—after all, we'd never been given any indication that Bishop Schofield was displeased by the ministry at San Andreas. On the Sunday after that ill-fated luncheon, I was to give the news to the parish that this would be my last Sunday as priest at St. Matthew's Church. Right then, the drums started beating in the hearts of parishioners of Saint Matthew's parish. We knew that our parish would be closed and the contents of our buildings taken, as had happened at Holy Trinity Church in Madera and Saint Dunstan's in Modesto, so sacred items and memorials began to be removed from the church and stored for safekeeping. Almost immediately, the parish gathered at the coffee hour to decide what action to take to be able to remain faithful Episcopalians and continue to witness to the Gospel of Jesus Christ in the San Andreas area. If we didn't have our building, we'd still gather as a parish and worship together.

Meanwhile, the bishop's canon to the ordinary came to the church the following Sunday to celebrate Mass and talk about the plans for St. Matthew's. The parish discussed two approaches to this visit: They would not allow the canon into the building, or they'd permit him to celebrate the Holy Eucharist but would not participate.

A faithful group of parishioners made an appointment to be heard on October 13 at Diocesan Council in Fresno, where the bishop would go against the diocesan canons and attempt to change St. Matthew's from parish to mission status in one swoop. Of course, our parishioners took a lawyer with them, which got the attention of the Diocesan Council and the bishop right away.

At the meeting, the parish was given unreasonable goals to meet within six months; if they failed to meet them, the parish would be reduced to mission status, and Bishop Schofield would be able to continue his plans for St. Matthew's. The unreasonable goals were to grow by fifty parishioners and to have enough money given to the church to support a full-time rector with benefits. These were unattainable goals because of the location of the parish in a rural foothill community. The financial goal was just a dream.

Within six months, though, St. Matthew's grew together more closely as a family than ever before. People became more active and faithful in their worship and proud of their heritage as Episcopalians. Cries of help were consistently made to The Episcopal Church leadership but it seemed as if those in New York weren't aware of what was actually happening within our diocese.

On December 8, 2007, at a meeting of Diocesan Convention at St. James' Cathedral in Fresno, Bishop Schofield rallied a majority of convention delegates to go into schism and leave the Episcopal Diocese of San Joaquin, and to form their own diocese apart from The Episcopal Church. This was heartbreaking to many who wanted to remain faithful within The Episcopal Church. Those who wished to remain faithful gathered at the Church of the Holy Family in Fresno to regroup, pray together, and consider what to do next as Episcopalians. Bishop John-David Schofield was deposed by the House of Bishops of The Episcopal Church a few months later, in March 2008.

From feelings of loss, grief, and mourning over what happened within our diocese, St. Matthew's has risen from that grave of survival mentality, to become a closer-knit, loving, and welcoming family, more aware of who we are and why we are here as we strive to witness to our faith in Jesus Christ and proclaim by our lives that all are welcome in God's church.

San Andreas, California
March 2011

Growing with Grace

Tim Vivian

The Reverend Dr. Tim Vivian is vicar of Grace Episcopal Church and a founding member of Remain Episcopal Bakersfield. He is also a professor of Religious Studies at California State University Bakersfield. Canonically resident in Los Angeles at the time, Tim had his license withdrawn by former Bishop Schofield for ministering to the LGBT community. When Grace was founded in 2008, he was appointed priest-in-charge by Presiding Bishop Katharine Jefferts Schori and was installed as vicar in 2009 by provisional Bishop Jerry Lamb.

As Bishop John-David Schofield moved toward schism in 2007, a group called Remain Episcopal formed in the northern part of the diocese and eventually opened a chapter in Bakersfield. About a dozen or so people met at the home of Larry and Pat Bentley late in 2006 and then fifteen or twenty met again at the Beale Library in January 2007.

That group then formed a house church that met weekly for worship and potluck on Sunday afternoons during the spring, summer, and fall at people's homes. Though

I'm an Episcopal priest and a member, I was not canonically certified in the diocese—Bishop Schofield had withdrawn my license—so we did not have Communion but read Evening Prayer together.

Later in 2007, knowing that the schism was imminent (the diocese voted the previous year to leave The Episcopal Church and would have a second vote in December, 2007), Remain Episcopal Bakersfield met in the chapel of First Congregational Church and celebrated Holy Communion. I celebrated and preached at that service.

Our group, about two dozen strong, met again on Epiphany Sunday 2008 and, again, I was the celebrant.

On January 24, 2008, the Reverend Canon Robert Moore, then of Seattle, who was appointed by The Episcopal Church's presiding bishop, the Most Reverend Katharine Jefferts Schori, as an interim pastoral presence in the San Joaquin Valley, spent the day in the greater Bakersfield area as part of a five-day "listening tour" that culminated in a Valley-wide conference in Hanford. An article on January 25 in the *Bakersfield Californian* reported Canon Moore's visit:

> At a Thursday night gathering of 60 to 70 believers and clergy at First Congregational Church and hosted by Remain Episcopal in the Diocese of San Joaquin, a faith community opposed to the split, Moore received hearty applause when he announced he had appointed the Rev. Tim Vivian, a Bakersfield resident, to a "temporary pastoral position as missionary priest under my direct supervision, which puts him within the jurisdiction of the presiding bishop of The Episcopal Church."
>
> Moore thus opened the way for Vivian to administer sacraments such as marriage, baptism, and

the Eucharist to local believers who don't have a parish to go to, as all three diocesan parishes in Bakersfield voted in favor of the split. Vivian is a Remain Episcopal member and a licensed priest canonically resident in Los Angeles, meaning he could perform priestly duties in that diocese but not in San Joaquin without proper licensing or consent.

"There's no bishop to license him" locally, Moore said, since Jefferts Schori formally declared on Jan. 11 that San Joaquin Bishop John-David Schofield, who led the diocesan split, had abandoned the communion of the Episcopal Church and "inhibited," or stopped, his duties as a bishop. Vivian's temporary assignment will cease "as soon as there is a new bishop," Moore said.

In 2008, the Most Reverend Jefferts Schori nominated the Right Reverend Jerry Lamb, retired bishop of the Episcopal Diocese of Northern California, as provisional bishop of the Episcopal Diocese of San Joaquin. In March 2008 delegates from the remaining Episcopal parishes unanimously elected Bishop Lamb as provisional. Bishop Lamb retired in March 2011 and the delegates and clergy elected the Right Reverend Chester Talton as the new provisional bishop.

On Sunday, November 16, 2008, Bishop Lamb installed me as vicar of Grace Episcopal Church. Grace was officially made a mission of the diocese at the first reconstituted Diocesan Convention in March 2008. On May 31, 2009, the Saturday before Pentecost, Bishop Lamb ordained Dr. Vern Hill, a former Methodist minister, as priest.

This coming All Saints' Day, Grace will celebrate its fourth anniversary in the chapel. The parish is now a fully functioning mission with a nine-member bishop's committee, senior warden, and junior warden, and two part-time clergy, Vicar Tim Vivian and Associate Vicar Vern Hill. As of March 2011, there are 141 parishioners, with an average Sunday attendance of 72 and active Sunday school and adult education programs. Among the paid parish staff are a choir director, a pianist, two child-care workers, and a youth director. We have numerous committees and groups, including stewardship, outreach, LGBT, Daughters of the King, Aging with Grace, a men's group, and a worship group. Serving our community are Eucharistic ministers who help with Sunday services, pastoral Eucharistic ministers who help with home visits and pastoral care, and acolytes.

Grace has grown slowly but steadily, as has its pledged income. Our budget in 2011 was $92,000, up from $72,000 in 2010. In 2010, Grace raised more than $13,000 for outreach.

Growth is hard to predict. About a third of the parish is composed of former Roman Catholics. Since Grace is the only welcoming and inclusive church within the Catholic tradition (Orthodox, Anglican, Roman), we anticipate more growth in this area. About 20 percent of parishioners identify as LGBT, including many couples with children.

We don't know how long we'll stay at First Congregational Church—that's partly up to our hosts. Although The Episcopal Church has prevailed in almost all its legal proceedings to regain the property and monies of the diocese, it's not clear when the cases will finally be settled and what will happen after that.

Grace currently pays First Congregational Church $1,000 a month for full use of the chapel and most other buildings on the FCC campus. They generously did not charge us for more than a year, and then introduced a gradual rent increase until it reached the current amount.

Grace has child care for youngsters less than four years of age, with two paid staff; Sunday school for kindergarten through grade six; Episcopal Youth Fellowship for middle- and high-schoolers, with a paid director; and an adult education program that includes a book group, speakers, catechism classes, and Lent and Advent soup suppers and programs. The youth director and I lead six-week confirmation and baptismal programs, usually once a year for confirmation and twice a year for baptisms.

What can Grace say about planting churches? It's hard work. But with parishioners like those at Grace, it is exciting and Spirit-filled work, too. The people of Grace founded the parish as an outreach and inclusive church, and we strive to maintain those principles.

Perhaps most important is that Grace practices mutual ministry, where *everyone* is a minister, not just the clergy. This is crucial to the founding, health, and growth of a parish.

Bakersfield, California
March 2011

The Joys

Jane Lamb

*"Happy are they who dwell in your house! They will al-
ways be praising you . . .
Happy are the people whose strength is in you! Whose
hearts are set on the pilgrim's way." Psalm 84, Book of
Common Prayer, p. 707*

As a child I heard stories of the horrors that the early Christians endured and I couldn't begin to comprehend that kind
of experience. I only knew wonderful, healthy parishes with
big signs out front advertising their existence and inviting
people to enter. Inside were warm Sunday school rooms;
clergy, choirs, and acolytes in beautiful robes; and many
nice people. The music always seemed glorious and I loved
singing in the junior choir. I was proud of my church and
felt safe and comfortable being a clergy kid, though I was
just a bit rebellious.

As I grew older and understood more of what early
Christians experienced, it was still nearly incomprehen-
sible. How and why would the Christians face such fear

and continue to struggle to worship God through Jesus the Christ? Could I ever experience such courage? Probably not, I thought, but it was old history and I was enjoying my church as it was. Even through the struggles of the changing church with women priests, a new Book of Common Prayer and a new Hymnal, the election of the first woman bishop and the election of the first openly gay bishop, I was content and felt secure. The church was dynamic and exciting.

My experience in the Diocese of San Joaquin between 2008 and 2011 was a profound one for me. Here were people who had the courage to say *no* and lose the physical ties to their faith, to remain in The Episcopal Church. After the split, the Episcopalians of that diocese had only seven church buildings to worship in. The continuing faith communities—congregations without a church building—had nothing to use in liturgical worship. The continuing Episcopal diocesan office did not have office space, much less office supplies—not even a stapler.

But about a thousand Episcopalians decided to stay true to The Episcopal Church and so the journey of survival began.

In the chapters of this book, clergy and laity have told their stories of the various hurts—betrayal, absolute authority, clericalism, censorship of information, fraud, isolation, spiritual hurt, ostracism, and greed. But with every hurt there is an accompanying joy.

With the financial, moral, and spiritual support of the Executive Council leadership and the presiding bishop's office, the Episcopal Diocese of San Joaquin has been able to survive. Gifts of vestments, prayer books, hymnals, Bibles, and all items needed for liturgical worship were sent to the diocese from other Episcopal churches in the United States. It was an outpouring of concern and support that lifted the hearts and diminished the pain of the remaining Episcopalians in San Joaquin. The five other dioceses in California—Northern California, California, El Camino Real, Los Angeles, and San Diego—rallied around with offers of support, education, and guidance.

At the first regular convention of the reconstituted Diocese of San Joaquin, a section of the parish hall at Church of the Savior in Hanford was set aside for a display of all of the gifts sent to the diocese from parishes and dioceses throughout the country. Each faith community had an opportunity to add to its meager church supplies.

Today, faith communities meet in a variety of places—a Jewish synagogue, a funeral home, an Odd Fellows Hall, and a historical society building used as a community theater, to name a few. And one parish, Trinity, Madera, was able to rent back its beloved church building that had been sold by the former, now deposed, bishop. The irony was not lost on the people of that church, but they felt it was still their church and they were happy to be "home."

The faith communities set up their worship space each week just before their service, wherever that might be, and after the service put the supplies away in their Church in a Box container until the next week. The fellowship of setting up and taking down their "church" each week has been a delight to behold. The congregations seem to have boundless energy and humor. But they also understand the seriousness of the situation, and they have taught me to appreciate the resilient human spirit.

By October 2010 the Diocese of San Joaquin had a total of twenty-one congregations—eight parishes and thirteen missions. The Episcopalians rediscovered the joy of their baptismal promises:

Will you continue in the apostles' teaching and fellowship, in the breaking of the bread and in the prayers?

Will you persevere in resisting evil, and whenever you fall into sin, repent and return to the Lord?

Will you proclaim by word and example the Good News of God in Christ?

Will you seek and serve Christ in all persons, loving your neighbor as yourself?

Will you strive for justice and peace among all people and respect the dignity of every human being?

And they could respond to each of these questions joyfully and confidently, proclaiming, "I will, with God's help."

These promises of how we will live our lives are at the core of who we are as humans and as Christians. These promises include everyone, not just the rich, the white, the straight, or the perfect. The remaining Episcopalians embraced their baptismal promises as a way to live their lives and to function as a diocese.

An example of their humor and resilience is the story of one faith community near the Mojave Desert. As I was waiting for the service to begin in a community center I began talking to a woman who was a long-time Episcopalian. She told me the story of the firing of the choir by the rector and the subsequent split from the church. My response was to say how very painful all of this must have been for the continuing Episcopalians. She responded with a chuckle, "Oh, we'll be all right; we have the two best cooks and half the choir!" Not a negative word was spoken but instead, energetic humor.

Being embraced by other people of faith, not only Episcopalians, was a source of comfort to the San Joaquin Episcopalians. They found great joy in belonging to The Episcopal Church and the wider religious community. One faith community was embraced by the members of a Jewish synagogue who opened their building on Sundays for the displaced Episcopalians. Others were hosted by a Congregational church and a Methodist church. Episcopalians throughout the country prayed for the health of the Episcopal Diocese of San Joaquin.

During the special convention when the first provisional bishop was installed, a new Standing Committee and Diocesan Council were elected, as were deputies to General Convention. Not one person elected to General Convention had ever been to one before. Only one person on either governing body had ever held a diocesan position. With the help of surrounding dioceses, the Standing Committee and Diocesan Council had a marvelous learning experience and both were competent in a short time. It helped also that their provisional bishop had nearly twenty years' experience in the episcopacy.

Finally, the diocese would experience the joy of checks and balances as the diocese became a diverse group of people sharing in decision making.

At the final meeting of the Remain Episcopal Steering Committee I observed a remarkable occurrence. The group was discussing how to proceed in the future. Of course, there was a variety of ideas and feelings. Throughout this hours-long meeting, all members' ideas were respected. If an idea was misunderstood or challenged it was done with utmost civility. It seemed as if Christians were participating in the meeting. It was a lovely dance of exchanging ideas and feelings with the ultimate resolution that Remain Episcopal would be of educational assistance to other dioceses and in

San Joaquin and should continue to exist. This group had been through a symbolic war together and they functioned like adults. What a treat to watch the joy of checks and balances in action.

At the regular Diocesan Convention in October 2008, the San Joaquin Episcopalians were introduced to many resources of The Episcopal Church, from which the diocese had been nearly isolated for nearly twenty years. The Cathedral Bookstore from the Diocese of Northern California brought many books, religious accoutrements, and badly needed supplies for sale.

The diocese had a monthly newspaper, *Episcopal Life San Joaquin*, affectionately called the *Wrap*, and Episcopalians also read *Episcopal Life* with its news of the wider church. Programs such as Fresh Start, Strength for the Journey, Pension Fund workshops, and clergy conferences designed to build collegiality were welcomed with enthusiasm. A CREDO experience for a number of people from the four continuing dioceses—Fort Worth, Pittsburgh, Quincy, and San Joaquin—provided a lifeline to the badly injured dioceses. The Episcopalians of San Joaquin now had a view of the broader church; they were no longer isolated. The joy of open communication was a lovely experience for everyone. At times it was so new and pleasurable that bluntness nearly pushed the envelope too far. The operative word is *nearly*; respect for one another was the unwritten rule.

At the Diocesan Convention of October 2008, a resolution was passed requiring an examination of the roles of those in the diocese who had not been able to enter all aspects of diocesan life, particularly women, people of color, and gay, lesbian, transgender, and bisexual people. A Commission on Equality was enacted. The commission

[1] http://diosanjoaquin.org/governance/equalcomm.html

worked hard and in October 2009 published its findings.[1] It was important to the Episcopal Diocese of San Joaquin to experience the joy of an acceptance of all God's children as full members of the diocese. To witness the comfort and delight and energy of those who previously had not been accepted as full members of the diocese was a deeply moving experience.

It was clear at the special convention of March 2008 that the laity wanted more involvement in all aspects of church leadership. As stated earlier, clericalism and absolute authority were the norm in the diocese. The clergy retained most of the power with the laity having little decision-making authority. The attendant joy was the joy of lay leadership and open elections. Again, with a Standing Committee and Diocesan Council with all but one member new to diocesan leadership, a whole new vista of ideas, vision, and energy infused the diocese.

Author Anne Lamott, in her 1995 book, *Bird by Bird*, writes, "You can safely assume that you've created God in your own image when it turns out that God hates all the same people you do." These words hit home when one thinks of the rigid limits that certain pious people place on God. The Episcopal Church strives to live out the promises we made at our baptism, not only the promises to continue to live a life dedicated to God in Christ but especially the promises to seek and serve Christ in all persons, loving our neighbors as ourselves and by striving for justice and peace among all people and respecting the dignity of every human being.

The Episcopal Church is often criticized within our denomination, as well as by other denominations, because we have been honest about, and accepting of, certain people whose lifestyle is not considered the norm by some. Yes, the church has warts, but don't we all? It is the joy of learning the wonders of the church, as well as accepting what others might consider warts, that make us who we are. We are a wide-tent religion that allows for questions, mistakes, and the acceptance of all God's children. It isn't always easy but we work hard at it.

A healthy diocese consists of spiritually healthy bishops, priests, deacons, and laity; a healthy Episcopal Church consists of spiritually healthy dioceses. The experience of the Diocese of San Joaquin is an example of a spiritually ailing diocese that could spoil the church for others. The Episcopal Church consists of bishops and clergy and laity sharing in a transparent decision process that is healthy. The health of every diocese is integral to the health of the wider church. It is learning the understanding of the diocese's health in the role of the health of the wider church that is a joy.

There was a joyful spiritual awakening in the reconstituted Episcopal Diocese of San Joaquin. Within six months, parish programs, supported by the diocese, started four classes of Education for Ministry (EfM), and two diaconal students started at Church Divinity School of the Pacific for the first time in recent memory. Within the second year the Reverend Suzy Ward was the first woman to be ordained a priest in the diocese; a diocesan altar guild began, and parishes were doing outreach. One faith community, one mission, and one parish sent people to Navajoland to help with clean-up and irrigation work. At the first regular Diocesan Convention, the delegates voted to send the offertory collection out of the diocese. At the special convention in March 2008, four women priests were licensed as the newly installed provisional bishop's first order of business. They are all either rectors or priests-in-charge. Episcopalians of San Joaquin are hungry for learning about their church and enthusiastic to grow.

A great joy has been watching and experiencing celebrating Christ with pennies. It sounds strange, but one can indeed have absolutely wonderful worship with a Church in a Box, counting every penny spent or saved, appreciating any gift regardless of the size, and appreciating the humor of peculiar situations. When we arrived at a faith community meeting in a community theater, the congregation was setting up "church." The senior warden's wife approached me and explained there was no curtain for the stage. The stage was set up as a mountain cabin complete with stacked beer cans and a roll of toilet paper flapping in the breeze. I told her not to worry; the bishop would be fine with the setup. The choir and clergy processed and we sang the opening hymn with gusto. At the end of the opening hymn, Bishop Lamb said to the congregation, "I've been to many worship centers and experienced many reredoses but I must say, this one is the most original!" We all laughed and then got down to worship, the reredos forgotten.

At the special convention of March 2008 we said the prayer attributed to Saint Francis in unison and it was said with a sense of oneness, intimacy, and understanding. The prayer was adopted by the reconstituted diocese and is used at all diocesan events. It is as follows:

Lord, make us instruments of your peace. Where there is hatred, let us sow love; where there is injury, pardon; where there is discord, union; where there is doubt, faith; where there is despair, hope; where there is darkness, light; where there is sadness, joy. Grant that we may not so much seek to be consoled as to console; to be understood as to understand; to be loved as to love. For it is in giving that we receive; it is in pardoning that we are pardoned; and it is in dying that we are born to eternal life.

The Episcopal Diocese of San Joaquin has welcomed its new provisional bishop, the Right Reverend Chet Talton, retired suffragan bishop of Los Angeles, and his wife, April. The diocese is no longer just surviving but has moved to a missionary mode by the grace of God and hard work.

Las Cruces, New Mexico
June 2011

Appendix

Timeline History of the Episcopal Diocese of San Joaquin

1579: Sir Francis Drake anchored at Drake's Bay. The Reverend Francis Fletcher held several services on the Pacific shore.

1607: First American church "first planted in Virginia in the year of Our Lord 1607, by representatives of the ancient Church of England."

1780: Maryland convention where the name "Protestant Episcopal Church" was first used.

1782: William White published an outline for organizing a national church that included both clergy and laity.

1783: Samuel Seabury elected first American Episcopal bishop in colonial America.

1784: Samuel Seabury ordained bishop at St. Andrew's Cathedral, Aberdeen, Scotland, maintaining apostolic succession.

1785: August 3, first ordinations of the Protestant Episcopal Church on American soil took place.

1808: Spanish Army Lieutenant Gabriel Moraga embarked upon a trip into the San Joaquin Valley looking for potential Spanish Mission sites.

1811: October 3, William Ingraham Kip born in New York City.

1835: Kip graduated from General Theological Seminary; ordained deacon in June and priest in October.

1840: Episcopalian settlers began moving to central California.

1850: August 25, Organization of St. John's Episcopal Church, Stockton.

1853: The Reverend William Ingraham Kip elected missionary bishop of California by House of Bishops and confirmed by the House of Clerical and Lay Deputies at General Convention of the Protestant Episcopal Church, October 1853. Bishop Kip became fifty-ninth Episcopal bishop with apostolic succession at his ordination.

The following is from *The Church Journal*, 1853, about Bishop Kip's ordination:

> The weather was exceedingly unpleasant during the early part of the morning, which made the congregation by no means as large as it would otherwise have been. But after the consecration of the Bishop, and as the Communion Office was proceeding, the clouds broke away, and a gleam of tinted sunshine fell upon the altar and lighted up the Sanctuary. This is beautifully illustrative of the history of the Church in California. Her beginnings have long been overcast with storms and clouds, overhung with darkness and gloom. But now that a Bishop has

been consecrated for her, and clergy will flock with him to labor in the desolate places of that spiritual wilderness, we doubt not but the clouds will ere long break, and roll away, and the All-glorious Sun of Righteousness will shine cheeringly upon a land bringing forth her increase.

1854: January, Bishop William Kip arrived in San Francisco, California.

1854: February 17, Bishop Kip visited Stockton, California. He noted about St. John's Episcopal Church:

There were about three hundred persons present. The number of Prayer Books produced, the nature of the responses produced, gave evidence of a degree of churchmanship which argued well for the founding of a strong congregation in this place.

1855: During the month of October, Bishop Kip journeyed through the San Joaquin Valley. The following is a quote from one of his letters, on Sunday, October 14:

I felt myself compensated for the toil and labor of reaching here, by the opportunity afforded of administering the solemn sacraments of our Church where they had never been witnessed before, and for the benefit of those who otherwise might not receive them from other hands for years.

1856: Bishop Kip elected diocesan bishop of the Episcopal Diocese of California.

1890: William Ford Nicolas ordained coadjutor bishop, Diocese of California.

1893: Bishop Kip died April 7, 1893, at the age of eighty-two.

1893: William Ford Nicolas became diocesan bishop of the Diocese of California.

1910: January, Convention of the Diocese of California, consent was given to a third division of the diocese.

1910: October, Episcopal Missionary Diocese of San Joaquin carved out of the Diocese of California by vote of General Convention.

1911: January 25, Louis C. Sanford ordained first bishop of the Missionary District of San Joaquin.

1911–1942: Louis C. Sanford, Bishop.

1944–1968: Sumner F.D. Walters, Bishop.

1968–1988: Victor M. Rivera, Bishop.
1976: July, General Convention passed a resolution declaring "no one shall be denied access to ordination."

1988–2008: John-David Schofield, bishop until deposed, March 12, 2008.

2003: July: General Convention, Minneapolis, Minnesota "...confirms not the first gay bishop, but first openly gay bishop."

2005: Diocese of San Joaquin attempts to modify its constitution.

2006: December, first vote by Diocese of San Joaquin to attempt to leave The Episcopal Church. Constitution and Canons of The Episcopal Church requires two votes one year apart for constitutional changes.

2007: December, second vote by Diocese of San Joaquin to attempt to leave The Episcopal Church.

2007: John-David Schofield inhibited by the presiding bishop.

2008: March 12, 2008, John-David Schofield deposed by House of Bishops for his repudiation of the doctrine, discipline, and worship of The Episcopal Church and abandonment of the Communion of the Church.

2008: First annual convention of the re-constituted Episcopal Diocese of San Joaquin. March 29, 2008, Bishop Jerry A. Lamb elected and installed first provisional bishop of the diocese.
2011: March 5, 2011, Bishop Chester Talton elected and installed as the second provisional bishop of the Episcopal Diocese of San Joaquin.

Resources

Book of Common Prayer, The. New York.: Church Hymnal Corp, 1979.

"Consecration of the Bishop of California." *The Church Journal.* November 3, 1853, Appendix.

The Episcopal Church Annual. Harrisburg, PA: Morehouse Publishing, 2009.

Episcopal clergy. Episcopal Diocese of San Joaquin. March 2008 through July 2011.
    Specifically: The Reverend Kathryn Galicia, The Reverend Canon Mark Hall, The Reverend Glenn Kanestrom, The Reverend Michele Racusin, The Reverend John Shumaker, The Reverend Dr. Tim Vivian, The Reverend Suzy Ward, and The Reverend Robert Woods.

Episcopal laity. Episcopal Diocese of San Joaquin. March 2008 through July 2011.
    Specifically: Marion Montgomery-Austin, Richard Jennings, Nancy Key, John Ledbetter, Cindy Smith, Juanita Weber, and Carolyn Woodall (Diaconal Candidate).

Fulwiler, Toby, and Alan R. Hayakawa. *The College Writer's Reference.* Upper Saddle River, NJ: Prentice Hall, 1999.

Guida, Angela Gayle. "We Remained Episcopal." Project thesis, Church Divinity School of the Pacific, May 10, 2010.

"History of St. John the Evangelist, Episcopal Church." *San Joaquin Historian*, Oct.-Dec. 1975.

"House of Bishops consents to deposition of John-David Schofield, William Cox." *American Anglican.* www.americananglican.org/house-of-bishops-consents-to-deposition-of-john-david/ March 12, 2008.

"House of Bishops Statement on Schofield, Cox." *Episcopal News Service*, March 12, 2008.

Kelley, D.O. *History of the Diocese of California, From 1849 to 1914.* San Francisco: Bureau of Information and Supply, 1915.

Kip, William Ingraham. *Early Days of My Episcopate.* New York: Thomas Whittaker. 1892.

Kip, William Ingraham. *A California Pilgrimage.* Ed. Louis Childs Sanford. Private subscription only. Fresno, 1921.

"Bishop William Ingraham Kip." Obituary, *The New York Times*, April 8, 1893.

"Protestant Episcopal Church." Classic encyclopedia. Based on the 11th edition of *The Encyclopedia Britannica*, 1911.

Remain Episcopal Notebook. Compiled by Remain Episcopal of the Diocese of San Joaquin, 2004.

Robinson, Bruce A. "Female Ordination in The Episcopal Church, USA (ECUSA)." Religious Tolerance. http://www.religioustolerance.org/femclrg14.htm, June 22, 2006.

Wilkerson, Todd. Scottish History Online. www.scotshistoryonline.co.uk/episcopal-church.html, Feb. 11, 2010.